TWAYNE'S WORLD AUTHORS SERIES

A Survey of the World's Literature

Sylvia E. Bowman, Indiana University

GENERAL EDITOR

FRANCE

Maxwell A. Smith, Guerry Professor of French, Emeritus
The University of Chattanooga
Former Visiting Professor in Modern Languages
The Florida State University

EDITOR

Maurice Maeterlinck

TWAS 342

Courtesy of the Belgian Consulate General, New York

Maurice Maeterlinck

Maurice Maeterlinck

By BETTINA KNAPP

Hunter College
and
The Graduate Center of the
City University of New York

TWAYNE PUBLISHERS
A DIVISION OF G. K. HALL & CO., BOSTON

Library of Congress Cataloging in Publication Data

Knapp, Bettina Liebowitz, 1926—
  Maurice Maeterlinck.

  (Twayne's world authors series, TWAS 342. France)
  Bibliography: p. 189-92.
  1. Maeterlinck, Maurice.
PQ2625.A6K5   848'.8'09   74-19147
ISBN 0-8057-2562-8

I should like to thank my research assistants at
the Graduate Center of C.U.N.Y.
Janet Moser
Philippe Méni
Dean Vasil

Contents

About the Author

Bettina L. Knapp is Professor of Romance Languages at Hunter College and the Graduate Center of C.U.N.Y. She received her B.A. from Barnard and her M.A. and Ph.D. from Columbia, and studied at the Sorbonne. She is the author of *Louis Jouvet, Man of the theatre; Louise Labé; Le Mirliton, A Novel Based on the Life of Aristide Bruant; Antonin Artaud, Man of Vision; Jean Genet; Jean Racine, Mythos and Renewal in Modern Theatre; Céline Man of Hate; Off-Stage Voices*, twenty-eight interviews with French dramatists, actors, and directors. She is co-author of *That Was Yvette* and translator of *Cymbalum Mundi*. She has published articles and reviews in *La Revue d' Histoire du Théâtre; Yale/Theatre; Yale French Studies; Kentucky Romance Quarterly; Drama and Theatre; Show; Nineteenth-Century French Studies; Dada and Surrealism; Books Abroad; French Review; Romantic Review*, etc. Dr. Knapp, the recipient of a Guggenheim Fellowship, is presently at work on a volume to be entitled *Dream and Image*.

Preface

"Maeterlinck's philosophy is like a temple in action; an image emerges from each stone, each image is a lesson. It does not constitute a system. It has no architecture with respect to form; it has volume, height, density. The superior regions of the spirit have plateaux as restful as the vastest of clearings. It is there that Maeterlinck entices us: what am I saying? He recreates them for his own use, for our use, via images, atoms, the most sensitive to our human organs." So wrote Antonin Artaud in 1923.

Maeterlinck's plays, essays, and poems are, indeed, spiritually oriented. They deal with the most fundamental problems facing man — those of life and death — in subdued, nuanced, and imagistic tones. Maeterlinck probes man's inner world: his dreams, desires, until he reaches those arcane regions. There he extracts the hidden riches of the soul, brings them to the light of consciousness, for readers and spectators to experience in their own subjective fashion.

Maeterlinck's theater has been variously labeled: a theater of silence, of stasis, of darkness, of the dream. His early dramas — (*The Intruder, The Blind, Pelléas and Mélisande*) — are all of these things. Yet, they go beyond such limited nomenclatures. In that they give primacy to ritual, myth, gesture, and the world of the occult, they may be looked upon as precursors to contemporary absurdist theater. In good Symbolist tradition — following the dictates of Baudelaire, Villiers de l'Isle Adam, and Mallarmé — symbols are the chief vehicles used in his dramas to arouse sensation, to breathe life into the ephemeral essences which people Maeterlinck's stage.

Unlike André Antoine's naturalistic "slice of life" or "peephole" theater, Maeterlinck's world is inhabited by mysterious and dreamy forces. Words and phrases, repeated at regular intervals during the performances, are designed to evoke sensations; the sets, stark in their simplicity, arouse man's fantasy world; the subdued light, cast in eerie hues, lends a tremulous and haunting note to the scene; sound effects, integrated into the body of the drama, are percepti-

ble manifestations of an atemporal force — an unknown and terrifying destiny which hovered over each of the protagonists.

Maeterlinck frequently had recourse to the fairy tale structure in
his plays. It best expressed his mystical ideations. Divested of
cultural accouterments, the fairy tale is the profoundest and
simplest expression of the collective unconscious. It brings forth a
world of feeling, not the rational thinking function. Audiences,
therefore, could respond viscerally, empathetically to a Maeterlinck
play, be emotionally stimulated or pained as the case might be.

May 17, 1893, was a date which made theatrical history. Lugné-
Poë, the future director of the famed Théâtre de l'Oeuvre, produced Maeterlinck's *Pelléas and Mélisande*. He had done away with
footlights, with a cluttered proscenium. Audiences, therefore,
viewed an almost bare stage. A single light cast dull grayish-blue
shadows from above, injecting the appropriate atmosphere of gloom
and mystery onto the stage happenings. Mélisande alone walked in
the lighted areas; the rest of the cast was in darkness. A gauze curtain hung between the stage and the audience, emphasizing still
further the remote and arcane nature of the protagonists amid the
web they were spinning throughout their life's course. The acting
was stylized, restrained. Lugné-Poë insisted on economy of gesture.
The voices rang out in subdued, atonal harmonies, like polyphonic
recitations of litanies. The spectacle took on the stature of a sacred
ritual.

With the passing of years, Maeterlinck altered his style. Realistic
and philosophical plays would better serve, he felt, as vehicles for
Georgette Leblanc's histrionic talents. His former ethereal, poetic,
childlike heroines were now transformed into *femmes fortes.*
Ariadne and Bluebeard, for which Paul Dukas wrote the musical
score, was the prototype of the feminist woman; *Monna Vanna*, the
political heroine, yielded her body to the enemy for the collective
good; *Mary Magdalene*, the religious martyr, accepted Christ's
crucifixion rather than give herself to the Roman officer who
desired her, convinced that her act was the highest and purest expression of divine love.

Maeterlinck's realistic-philosophical dramas were contrived. They
lacked the intensity, the poetry and the authenticity of his early
works. Of the twenty dramas he wrote after his Symbolist phase,
only *The Blue Bird* is of superior quality. Here again he reverted to

the fairy tale dimension, to the world of the child.

As an essayist, Maeterlinck treated a vast range of subjects: entomology, philosophy, war, religion, mathematics, physics, psychometrics. Though his essays are discursive, loosely organized, and frequently repetitious, his inquiries into nature are both moving and technically accurate. Maeterlinck had raised bees as a young man, as had his father, and was familiar with nearly every aspect of the bee. His love for the bee — and for most animals, with the exception of the cat and the termite — bears witness to his sense of oneness with his natural surroundings.

Maeterlinck's religious and metaphysical speculations are also of great interest. Deeply influenced by such Neoplatonists as Plotinus, Boehme, and Ruysbroeck, Maeterlinck formulated his own credo and he rejected all organized religions. An agnostic and pantheist, he did not believe in a creator God. His God was unknown, omniscient, omnipotent — beyond man's comprehension. Maeterlinck's God, like that of the mystics whose works had so deeply impressed him, was embedded in the all. "God is the universe which is before anything else infinite space and time in its unlimited form: eternity," he wrote in *The Great Fairyland*. To try to understand God, to transpose His wishes, as the organizers of revealed religion claim to have done, is to reduce the infinite to the finite. God may be experienced from within, Maeterlinck asserted; He will never be revealed.

The Great Secret, Maeterlinck's historical study of occultism, including Vedic teachings, the secrets of both Osiris and Zoroaster, and the writings of the pre-Socratics, Neoplatonists, and Hebrew Kabbalists, is fascinating. The same may be said for his volume on psychometrics, *The Unknown Host*. Transmission of thoughts, extrasensory perception, premonitory dreams, synchronicity, communication with the dead, and other experiences dealing with psychic phenomena are investigated with objectivity. That Maeterlinck should have been drawn to such parapsychological domains is comprehensible since so much research work was being accomplished during the 1920's and 1930's in these fields. What is startling, however, is the fact that scientists were also studying this area, which had heretofore been relegated to the world of religion, mysticism, or plain superstition. The schism between science and metaphysics, which had come to a head in the late nineteenth century, had ended. The work carried on by such people as Einstein, Adrian Dobbs, Sir John Eccles, to mention but a few, attests to this fact. Maeterlinck's volumes on the occult sciences served to heal the breach, to popularize the affinity between science, metaphysics, and psychometrics. Today, scientist and metaphysician can work together.

Maeterlinck's creative talents consist, wrote Antonin Artaud, "in his gift to reveal obscure sensations, unknown relationships of thought through images." His is a lasting contribution!

BETTINA L. KNAPP

Chronology

and Mélisande.

1896   *The Treasury of the Humble,* essay that causes his first rift with Georgette.

       Aglavaine and Sélysette, written for Georgette. The first of his new-style dramas.

1901.   *The Life of the Bee,* a scientifically accurate essay on bee culture.

       Ariadne and Bluebeard, a feminist play.

1902   *Sister Beatrice,* a liturgical drama. *Monna Vanna,* a political heroine.

1903   *Joyzelle,* influenced by Shakespeare's *Tempest,* fails.

1904   *The Double Garden,* an essay dealing for the most part with animals.

1907   *The Intelligence of Flowers* published, an essay on horticulture.

1909   *The Blue Bird* performed at the Moscow Art Theatre under the direction of Stanislavski. Maeterlinck's translation of *Macbeth* perfomed at the Abbey of St. Wandrille.

1911   Maeterlinck wins the Nobel Prize for Literature.

1913   *Death,* an essay written in 1911, is placed on the Index by the Catholic Church.

1914   World War I. Maeterlinck writes articles, tracts, gives speeches for Allies.

1917   *The Burgomaster of Stilmonde,* a war-propaganda drama.

1919   Marries Renée Dahon on February 15. Awarded honorary degree of Doctor of Law from Glasgow University.

       The Maeterlincks arrive in New York City on December 24. They return to France May 1920.

1920   Receives rank of Grande Croix in the Ordre de Léopold in Belgium.

1921   *The Great Secret,* a history of the occult sciences.

1922   *The Betrothal,* a sequel to *The Blue Bird.*

1927–   Maeterlinck publishes twelve volumes of essays on en-
1942   tomology, mysticism, science, and psychometrics.

1939   The Maeterlincks settle in Portugal. Given the medal of the Order of St. James of the Sword.

1940   *The Priest Setubal* is performed in April at the Theatre Nacional in Lisbon.

       The Maeterlincks arrive in New York on July 12.

1947   Arrives in Marseilles on August 10. Returns to his home in Nice.

1949   Maeterlinck dies of a heart attack on May 6. An agnostic, he requested no religious ceremony. A civil ceremony was performed; his body was cremated.

CHAPTER 1

The Formation of the Artist

I   *The Early Years*

HEAVYSET and robust, Maeterlinck radiated strength. His broad face, slightly pug nose, sensual lips, almond-shaped eyes, and large forehead gave the impression of a man of the world — sure of himself and outgoing. Maeterlinck was one to indulge in the sensual pleasures of life: fine wines and food. He considered mealtime sacred and refused to be interrupted during such rituals. Women also filled a powerful need in his life. Here too he gave vent to his feelings.

But there was another side to Maeterlinck, difficult to discern at times, which accounted perhaps for the negative impression he made on those who knew him only casually: self-centered, unfeeling, phlegmatic. Maeterlinck was a recluse. Wistful, timid, and withdrawn, he was never at ease with people. He shied away from them, from public affairs, from notoriety. He looked toward his shadowy inner world for solace, that impalpable region of halftones and reverie. There too he found inspiration.

Unlike his masters, the Symbolist poets — Baudelaire, Mallarmé, and Villiers de l'Isle Adam — Maeterlinck felt little or no antagonism between the outer and inner domain. Neither worked against the other; neither ushered in feelings of disgust or disdain for the bourgeois, the materialist, or the emerging industrial class. No conflict existed between spirit and flesh. Maeterlinck juxtaposed both worlds — gliding into or out of one at will — each working in harmony with the other. Whenever the balance grew shaky, whenever the world of illusion impinged too deeply upon the domain of reality, his essentially solid nature redressed the lack of equilibrium, enabling him to pursue his activities with relative ease.

Maeterlinck was sound in body and in mind — a rarity, seemingly, for the creative artist.

Maurice Maeterlinck[1] was born in Ghent, the capital of Flanders,
on August 29, 1862. A somber, sunless city, Ghent could boast of a
long and painful history. Wars and occupations by Charles V, Louis
XIV, Marlborough, and Louis XV had made of Ghent a European
battleground. Its cultural life, as revealed in certain monuments
which date back to the early Middle Ages, was remarkable. The
Cathedral of St. Bavon, begun in the tenth century and completed
in the sixteenth, housed Jean Van Eyck's world-famous painting
"The Adoration of the Lamb." Tourists were forever flocking to see
Ghent's city hall with its fourteenth-century façade and the church
of St. Nicolas that dates back to the twelfth century. Industries of all
sorts dotted the city: cotton and linen factories, which manufac-
tured damasks, wools, and laces, copper and iron foundries, sugar
refineries. All these added to the wealth of Ghent.

The Maeterlincks could trace their family tree back six centuries.
They were strictly Flemish stock; no Walloon, no French blood.

Maeterlinck's father, Polydore, was a notary who had worked
hard as a youth and had retired by the time his children were born.
He lived on his income. His only worries revolved around proper in-
vestments. Collecting rents from his tenants, investing in commercial enterprises, and tending to his bees and plants occupied his
days. A source of pleasure for Polydore was the construction and
continuous refurbishing of greenhouses on his property. He loved
flowers and experimented with them. A new type of flower was
even named after him. Intellectually Polydore had little to offer.
Rarely did he read a book. Still less was he interested in philosophy.
With regard to Catholic dogma, he could be called a liberal. According to his son, it was Polydore who helped him overcome the fears
concerning hell and purgatory the priests had inculcated in him.[2]
Maeterlinck describes his father as a strict, authoritarian, "tyran-
nical man" who "wore the mask of a dictator, but whose heart was
warm enough to soften wax."[3]

Father and son had little in common. Polydore looked upon the
career of a writer, of a creative artist, as unworthy. Business and
money matters were the only respectable *métiers*. Other differences

also separated Polydore and his son. Maeterlinck's father — as was the custom — indulged in liaisons with seamstresses, governesses, and pretty young girls. Maeterlinck remembered his mother forever hiring and firing the English and German governesses employed to care for her children because of her husband's interested eye. On one occasion, father and son shared the same woman's favors.

Maeterlinck's mother, Mathilde Colette Françoise Van den Bossche, was the daughter of a wealthy lawyer. Tender and gentle, she not only had the affection of her four children (three boys, Ernest, Oscar, Maurice, and one girl, Marie) but of her husband as well. Though not interested in cultural events, Mme. Maeterlinck understood her son's literary needs and his creative spirit. It was she who helped him both financially (by lending him money to print his first book of poetry) and psychologically (by encouraging him in his undertakings).

When the children were still young, the Maeterlincks bought a small white house with green shutters at Oostacker, right on the Dutch frontier, where they spent their summer months. There was plenty of room to run about, to exercise, fish, and swim. The Maeterlincks' lawn went almost down to the Terneuze canal, which led from Ghent to Holland and then out to sea.[4] "It looked as if the ships from Liverpool and London passed right through the garden," Maeterlinck wrote.[5] Water surrounded the Maeterlincks very nearly on all sides. It is not surprising then that such a liquid atmosphere should have impressed him so deeply and figured so frequently as a central symbol in his writings for years to come. Maeterlinck recalls a frightening experience he had as a child, when he almost drowned in the canal. Had it not been for his father's quick thinking and a carpenter's strong arms, he would have drowned.[6]

It was at Oostacker too that Maeterlinck wrote his first plays. He was nine or ten at the time. He had found a copy of Molière's works in his grandmother's house and decided to adapt *The Doctor in Spite of Himself, Scapin's Deceits* and *The Hypochondriac* for the stage, omitting what he considered to be the monotonous romantic episodes and stressing the slapstick, beating, and satiric scenes.[7] Friends and relatives were invited to applaud the artistry of the budding playwright. His father, however, unfamiliar with Molière's plays and fearing that unseemly words would be used, put a halt to such enterprises.

Maeterlinck's schooling was conventional. At the age of six he was sent to a girls' convent school that accepted boys up to the age of seven — the Sisters of the Nouveau Bois. There he learned his prayers, catechism, religious history, and the rudiments of mathematics. Lithographs depicting events in both the Old and New Testaments hung on the walls. Maeterlinck claimed that he never tired to look at these reproductions because there was something about them that appealed to his fancy.

A year later, in 1869, Maeterlinck entered the Institut Calamus. The headmaster, Maeterlinck recalled, was the prototype of all headmasters: his thick glasses rested on an acquiline nose, his high false collar gave him an air of rigidity and his priestly look inspired the children with awe.[8] After the first fight with the school bully, Maeterlinck, who came out the loser, was withdrawn from the institute and sent, in September 1874, to the Jesuit College of Sainte-Barbe in Ghent.

Maeterlinck underwent "seven years of narrow tyranny," he wrote, as a student in this Jesuit college. The lugubrious and joyless existence, the extreme discipline, the excoriating stories of damnation he was constantly told destroyed whatever fun he might have had as a boy. The Fathers were forever reminding the students of the temptations of the flesh — sin and damnation. "If they had not spoken of it," Maeterlinck asserted, "we would never have thought of them."[9] The sermons revolved around hell, burning, corporeal punishment. The anguish he experienced at this period centered around the "seduction of the flesh." The terror of damnation discouraged the children from ever changing their shirts or underclothes. One of the students was so tormented at the thought of thinking about or of looking at his own mother, for fear some evil associations might be aroused within him, that he lived in a state of panic. The dirt, the ugliness of the surroundings were repugnant to the young and "clean" Maeterlinck. "Their church was an ignominious masterpiece which made me suffer as a butterfly must suffer when enclosed in a garbage pail."[10] The walls of Sainte-Barbe — "the prison," as Maeterlinck called it — were covered with gluey dirt, "the dishes and glasses, the eating utensils were so greasy that they slid through one's fingers like eels."[11] The teachers, however, believed they were acting in good faith. They were patient and devoted to the students — simply misguided.

Maeterlinck could not stand the bigotry of the Fathers. There were too many no's and too few yes'es. The works of the French Romantic poets were forbidden; nor was verse writing permitted. Music was not taught. Plays were ruled out, except those concerning religious subjects. Freedom of expression and thought were out of the question. What Maeterlinck despised above all, and for which he never forgave the Jesuit Fathers, were the negative ramifications of this kind of instruction. "There is only one crime which cannot be forgiven, that of having poisoned the joys and destroyed the smile of a child."[12] The seven years he spent with the Jesuit Fathers left their mark on him; it accounted perhaps in part for his antagonism and distaste for the Catholic Church in particular and for organized religion in general.

Nevertheless, there was a positive side to his educational experience. He met and became friendly with two young men interested in the literary world: Charles Van Lerberghe and Grégoire Le Roy, also students at the Jesuit College. Although the three had different temperaments — Van Lerberghe lived in a world of dreams and was strictly unrealistic, whereas Le Roy was down to earth — they became inseparable.

The three had great hopes for the future. They reasoned that the poet Georges Rodenbach, the author of *The Foyer of Fields* (1877), among other volumes of poems and plays, had gone to Sainte-Barbe College.[13] So had Emile Verhaeren, who was to win international fame with *The Flemish* (1883) and books of verse.

Belgium in the 1880's was experiencing a kind of literary *renovatio*. The magazine *La Jeune Belgique*, edited by Max Waller, was founded in 1881 and flew the Parnassian banner of art for art's sake. Poetry and literature, therefore, had no political or economic mission. It was to be written for the beauty it could evoke or the spirituality it encouraged. *La Jeune Belgique* was to publish Maeterlinck's first poem, "Les Joncs" ("The Rushes"), on November 1, 1883. Though his first verses could be labeled servile, an almost puerile imitation of Parnassian masters, the publication of his poem encouraged him. Other periodicals were also founded during this period. *L'Art Moderne*, founded in 1881, edited by Edmond Picar and Octave Maus, was politically oriented at first. Later it accepted the works of Symbolist poets. *La Wallonie*, started in

1886 by Albert Mockel, could boast of Mallarmé, Gide, and Valéry among its contributors.

Although Maeterlinck had opted for a literary career, his father forced him to study law. He enrolled at the Ghent University Law School and despised every moment he devoted to his studies. Law was a "parroting" procedure, he later wrote. All that has to be done is to take down the teachers' lectures, then learn them by heart. The exams were easy and consisted of writing on paper what had been committed to memory.[14] In June of 1885, Maeterlinck became a doctor of law. He then persuaded his father that a trip to Paris and exposure to the Palais de Justice with its famous barristers would do much to broaden his legal education. Polydore acquiesced.[15] He agreed to subsidize his son's trip and his living expenses for five or six months. Maeterlinck arrived in Paris in October 1885. Charles Van Lerberghe and Georges Le Roy joined him there, ostensibly for the same purpose — to perfect their knowledge of legal matters. The three lived in a small apartment on the rue de Seine. Maeterlinck visited the Parisian law courts five or six times during his stay. Almost immediately, however, he concluded that there was little difference between Belgian and French legal orators: both were dull and uninspiring.[16]

How could one study law in Paris in 1885? A city burgeoning with creativity — the mecca of the arts?

The Impressionists were fighting hard to make a name for themselves in the visual arts. Cézanne, Monet, Pissarro, Degas, Seurat, Sisley, Signac, and Gauguin rejected the realism and materialism of the conventional painters of their time. They opted for canvases splashed with light, air, color. Let imagination reign free, they felt; Baudelaire had labeled imagination "the queen of faculties." The Impressionists chose to depict form via suggestion, nuances. To arouse the senses was their goal. Cézanne had just completed what was to become the famous canvas "House on a Hill" (1885); Monet, "The Haystack at Giverny" (1884); Gauguin, "Still Life" (1885); and a bit earlier, Pissarro, "Road to Pontoise in Osny" (1883); Renoir "Dame at Boujival" (1883); Sisley, "Fields at Veneux-Nadon" (1881). Van Gogh had recently arrived in Paris.

The independent painters were disgruntled with the official judges and their galeries. Cézanne, Pissarro, Monet and the others refused to yield to the abuses and retrogressive ways of the popular artists of their time. In 1884 they founded the "Société des Artistes Indépendants" and wrote, "This society stands for the suppression of juries and seeks to help artists to freely present their work before the bar of public opinion."[17] That same year the Salon des Indépendants gave its first exhibit — hanging canvases by Signac and Ensor, and including studies of what was to become Seurat's "La Grande Jatte."[18]

In the domain of poetry, Symbolism was in its heyday. Baudelaire's *Flowers of Evil* had inspired creative writers to reach beyond the world of reality — to immerse themselves through the senses in a transcendental sphere that would put them in touch with the entire cosmos. Poetry must evoke, suggest, symbolize. Metaphors, analogies, images, and symbols would be the vehicles through which the writer would be able to concretize amorphous feelings and moods.

Rimbaud — the nineteenth-century Prometheus, the fire-stealer as he was to be called — shocked the literary world with his violent, hallucinatory, and distorted visions that made up the bulk of his *Season in Hell* and *Illuminations*. He advocated a savage rebellion, a concerted disorientation of the senses. The poet is a visionary, a seer, he declared; poetry is a mystic revelation. At the age of twenty, Rimbaud had given the world his greatest works, and by 1880 he had already left for Africa. His literary career had come to an end.

Verlaine, the author of imagistic and melancholy verse, felt most acutely the conflict between flesh and spirit. He longed for God; but instead of finding a way to assuage his despair, he turned to alcohol. He grew sick, degrading himself as the years passed. His talent lapsed.

The dean of French Symbolists, Stéphane Mallarmé, received young poets on Tuesdays in 1884. They discussed the latest trends in the literary world and works in progress. Mallarmé despised the ugliness of the industrial civilization, of which he was a part, and longed to experience cosmic consciousness. His poetry was hermetic, a distillation of complex thoughts he enclosed in words, unusual and revolutionary syntactical procedures. "The Afternoon of a Faun" (1876) and "Hérodiade" were constructed around a focal idea or symbol, a metaphor which was then developed via a series of evocations. Mallarmé's works were enigmatic, obscure; they captivated by the sheer beauty of the visual and musical evocations, by the density of the thoughts.

The young Jules Laforgue, labeled a "Decadent," had just published his "Complaints" (1885). Disenchanted and sick, he meditated on the cruelty of life and likened himself to the suffering buffoon. Laforgue was an innovator; disassociating images and feelings, expressing thoughts in a willfully chaotic disorder, using neologisms, juxtaposing rare and common words, he injected his verse with a fresh quality. He died in 1887 of tuberculosis, at the age of twenty-seven.

Villiers de l'Isle Adam, Mallarmé's close friend, author of poetry and short stories, was more than anyone else to make a profound impression on Maeterlinck. "Villiers de l'Isle Adam, the providential man, at the right time and I don't know by what stroke of fate was to orient and fix my destiny,"[19] Almost nightly Maeterlinck and his friends met Villiers at a brasserie in Montmartre. There they talked for hours on end. Villiers treated them as friends, "as equals," though they were unknowns. Villiers was poor, terribly so; his clothes were threadbare. Yet, Maeterlinck wrote later, he walked with dignity, like a "provisionally dethroned king."[20] Villiers' voice was arresting, hypnotic, "white, cottony, stifled, and already similar to a voice from beyond the tomb, he 'spoke' to us about his works which were to be born."[21] On certain occasions Villiers read from his *Cruel Tales*, at other times from his mystical play *Axel* which had just been published in a periodical. Maeterlinck described his readings as a "mystery" unfolding, as though "secret masses" were being "celebrated in hushed tones."[22] Maeterlinck and his friends looked upon themselves as "officiants or accomplices to some pious or sacrilegious ceremony." And when it was all over, at around one in the morning, he and his friends would accompany Villiers back to his home, then make their way back to their rooms, "crossing the now silent Paris peopled only with shadows." They were excited, stimulated by Villiers, this "indefatigable magician," this "inexhaustible visionary."[23]

Villiers did not live in the workaday world. He could not adapt to it. His realm was that of the occult, of the fable. He believed in the powers of Merlin, the magician, in the existence of Tristan and the Knights of the Holy Grail. These heroes of some remote and fantastic past were his reality. He despised the materialism, the positivism, and scientific attitudes of his century; the ugliness he saw about him, the bourgeois society, a prelude, he said, to man's future degradation. Villiers' world was metaphysical. He delved into hypnosis, magnetism, premonitory visions, and metempsychosis. A student of the *Zohar*, of alchemy, Orphism, and a friend of Edouard Schuré, the author of *Great Initiates*, his writings abound in extraworldly themes. Like the philosophers and mystics of the Renaissance (Kepler, Paracelsus, Nicholas de Cusa, Giordano Bruno), Villiers was convinced that the universe was a living being, possessed by a soul, and that the world of phenomenon, or differentiated reality, was merely an emanation of this single force. Nothing was isolated, therefore, in the world, no gesture was unique; every movement, every breath had repercussions, reverberations; all was linked via universal sympathies.

Joris Karl Huysmans was likewise a student of the occult. The author of *Against the Grain* (1884), which Arthur Symons called "the breviary of decadence," he studied Satanism and its rituals in the France of his day. He too despised mediocrity and the reality engulfing him. As a "Decadent," he longed for an artificial and exotic world and spent his hours analyzing and dissecting his feelings, sensations and memories. It was he who introduced the works of the fourteenth-century Flemish mystic Jean Van Ruysbroeck to Maeterlinck. Six years later, when Maeterlinck translated Ruysbroeck's *The Adornment of Spiritual Marriage* (1891) from the original Flemish into French, he sent Huysmans the volume with the following inscription: "To Joris Karl Huysmans, to the profoundly admired master who set me on the path to Ruysbroeck."[24]

When Maeterlinck returned to Ghent, exhilarated by his months in Paris, he found his legal career still more dissatisfying. Yet, a dutiful son, he continued the practice of law and accepted the financial support of his father as well as the clients his relatives had recommended to him.

A year after his return to Ghent, in 1886, Maeterlinck made his way back to Paris. Le Roy, Van Lerberghe, and new friends Paul Roux (later known as Saint-Pol Roux), Pierre Quillard, René Ghil, Rodolphe Darzens, and others inaugurated a literary magazine, *La Pléïade*, Maeterlinck's narrative "Le Massacre des Innocents"

("The Massacre of Innocents") appeared in this short-lived periodical in May, and six of his poems in June.

"The Massacre of the Innocents" is a transposition of art. This genre was not new. It had been successfully used by Baudelaire, Gautier, Flaubert, and Huysmans before him. Maeterlinck's narrative was inspired by Breughel's painting "The Massacre of the Innocents." He transposed the action from the Holy Land to a Flemish village in the Middle Ages. The Spanish soldiers who occupied the area at the time organized a systematic campaign to kill every child in the town. They cut off children's heads, hanged them, tortured them, piercing their bodies with lances, and "when all the children had been killed, the tired soldiers wiped their swords in the grass and had supper under the pear tree afterwards."

Maeterlinck's story was not merely written for aesthetic reasons. It had philosophical ramifications which Maeterlinck would amplify with the passing of years. If God is good, as church doctrine claims, how is it that He permits such injustices to take place in His world? What crimes have the innocent children committed against Him? or anyone? Will such carnage continue increasing in horror as man becomes more civilized?

Two years later Maeterlinck's second short story, "Onirologie" ("Onirology"), was printed in *La Revue Belge*. It was inspired no doubt by the tales of two authors he greatly admired: Poe and Hawthorne. "Onirology" relates an experience about a strange vision. The protagonist of the story, a young man living in America, had no information concerning his origins, his family. One night in a dream he sees a strange town, unusual countrysides, and experiences unfamiliar sensations. Later in life he comes upon documents concerning his birth and heritage. These lead him to Utrecht. Upon arrival in this city he is traumatized by what he sees: the very decor of his dream. "Onirology" is an example of Maeterlinck's interest in the occult, a fascination which will develop in depth with the passing of time.

Maeterlinck was leading a double life. By day he worked as a lawyer and the rest of the time wrote short stories and verse. His lack of financial independence may account for the fact that he did not take the final step to give up the law. He did decide, however, to publish a volume of poetry in 1889, *Serres Chaudes* ("Hothouses"), at his own expense. He knew only too well that poetry is not a profitable source of income and so did not contact a commercial publisher.[25] His mother, unbeknown to his father, permitted him to use his savings; his brother and sister also gave their hard-saved sous to him, charging a rather high rate of interest on the loan. Grégoire Le Roy offered Maeterlinck a hand in running the printing press owned by a mutual friend. The future sculptor Georges Minnes also came to Maeterlinck's aid.[26] One hundred fifty-five copies were printed; only a few of these were sold in Brussels. Maeterlinck's *entrée* into the literary world was uneventful to say the least.

Maeterlinck explains his choice of title in the following manner: "This title, Hothouses, imposed itself naturally because Ghent is the town of the horticulturalist, and of floriculture even more so, where cold, warm, and hothouses abound."[27] The word "hothouse," however, takes on a broader connotation as one reads through Maeterlinck's verses. It reflects his profound *ennui*, his spleen, which weighs him down with lassitude. Bound, constricted, he experiences the dull sensation of emptiness, resulting from his incarceration in a limited atmosphere. The dank, dismal, and suffocating air of the hothouse certainly mirrors Maeterlinck's own inner world. Yet despite the lethargy, the feelings of stasis expressed in the verses, hothouses have their positive sides. Because of their enclosed structure and warm temperature, hothouses protect seeds, help them sprout, give them sustenance and the strength which might have otherwise been drained from them by the rigors of the outside world. Within the hothouse, then, there live inchoate both the forces of destruction and construction — a *complexio oppositorum*.

Through *Hothouses* introduced neither new themes nor images, there was a freshness and an authenticity in his subjective approach to the claustrophobic atmosphere of his environment, which permeated every particle of his being. In his poem "Feuillage du Coeur" ("Foliage of the Heart") we read:

> Sous la cloche de cristal bleu
> De mes lasses mélancolies,
> Mes vagues douleurs abolies
> S'immobilisent peu à peu:

Under the crystal blue bell
Of weary melancholia,
My vague torments abolished
Are immobilized little by little:

In "Orison" we penetrate Maeterlinck's religious world; we listen
to his doubts, his conflicts droning on like a litany.

Vous savez, Seigneur, ma misère!
Voyez ce que je vous apporte!
Des fleurs mauvaises de la terre,
Et du soleil sur une morte.

You know of my misery, Lord!
See what I bring you!
Bad flowers from the earth,
And some sun on a dead one.

The repetitions of words, images, and sonorities, the protracted
silences, the imperceptible tonal nuances ushering in soulscapes
tinged with discord, the variety of color ranges and the emotional
impact they inject into the verses enshroud them with a dreamy atmosphere that is broken up, at times, with the intrusion of more
aggressive feelings. In the poem "Hothouses," Maeterlinck seems
to cry out his anger:

Mon Dieu! mon Dieu! quand aurons-nous la pluie,
Et la neige et le vent dans la serre!

My God! my God! when will we have rain,
And snow and wind in the hothouse!

Dissatisfaction and a mood of restlessness are encroaching on the
hermetically sealed atmosphere of the hothouse!

II   Princess Maleine — "A Masterpiece"

Maeterlinck wrote a play, *La Princesse Maleine*. It would, he
hoped, reach more readers than his volume of verse. Although it
was first printed in serial form in a Brussels review, *La Société
Nouvelle*, Maeterlinck insisted it appear in a volume. Under no il-

lusions concerning the possibilities of having a commercial publisher undertake such a hazardous venture, he once again had recourse to his mother. He knew she refused her children nothing.[28] By juggling her monthly budget, Mme Maeterlinck saved 250 francs which she gave to her son. The play appeared in print in December 1889.[29]

Princess Maleine takes place in a northern land, in some vague era. Maleine is affianced to Prince Hjalmar, whose father, the king, is senile. After a misunderstanding between the king and Princess Maleine's parents, she is taken home and locked in a tower, but she escapes. After wandering through forests and countrysides, she arrives at Hjalmar's castle and enters disguised, only to learn that her fiancé is now betrothed to Uglyane, the daughter of Queen Anne of Jutland. Queen Anne, who dominates the doddering king, discovers Maleine's identity and decides to kill her. The mentally deficient king agrees to the undertaking; Maleine is strangled. Prince Hjalmar's grief is so great he stabs first Queen Anne and then himself.

As a symbolistic drama, *Princess Maleine* incarnates the worlds of nightmare and joy, the inexorable march of fate and man's feeble attempts to circumvent destined misfortunes. *Princess Maleine* may also be considered a dramatic fairy tale. A fairy tale concretizes an earthly experience. It enables feeling to take precedence over the rational.[30]

The fairy tale, which is the *prima materia* of most of Maeterlinck's early plays, may be defined in the following manner:

Fairy tales are the purest and simplest expression of collective unconscious psychic processes. Therefore their value for the scientific investigation of the unconscious exceeds that of all other material. They represent the archetypes in their simplest, barest, and most concise form. In this pure form, the archetypal images afford us the best clues to the understanding of the processes going on in the collective psyche. In myths or legends, or any other more elaborate mythological material, we get at the basic patterns of the human psyche through an overlay of cultural material. But in the fairy tales there is much less specific conscious cultural material and therefore they mirror the basic patterns of the psyche more clearly.[31]

In ancient times, in Greece in particular, fairy tales were told to adults and to children alike; they were considered a "spiritual occupation."[32] Not until the eighteenth century — the Age of Enlightenment — when reason was believed to be the *sine qua non* of all knowledge, and therefore life's goal, was the fairy tale relegated to the children's world and fantasy driven underground. Though certain storytellers in the eighteenth century tried to rehabilitate what was considered naïve and unrealistic, it was not until Cazotte and Nodier, that the world of enchantment again gained credence. A long line of fanciful works followed, written by Hoffmann, Novalis, Nerval, Gautier, Villiers de l'Isle Adam, and others. The realm of mystery and of the intangible answered a particular need in man, and the burgeoning of such tales evidenced a desire to render less potent a growing power of reason in a scientifically oriented world.

The fairy tale enabled Maeterlinck to exteriorize his subjective world in structured patterns. Inherent in the fairy tale form is (1) a sense of timelessness, (2) an archetypal aspect to the *dramatis personae*, and (3) frequent use of a variety of symbols. These characteristics are implicit in *Princess Maleine*.

1. Timelessness. Linear time has been abolished. *Princess Maleine* takes place in some nebulous past, probably during the medieval period when forests, castles, and large bodies of water dotted the northern landscapes; where vast land masses and high mountain ranges were barely discernible so thick was the fog, an atmosphere portending fear.

The variety of color tones woven into Maeterlinck's text (the bottle greens, the grays, the blacks) injects a cyclical quality into the play, divesting it still further of any fixed time scheme. Like the canvases of Jacob Solomon van Ruysdael, "A Village Near the Dunes" and "The Ferry Boat," with their tiny figures silhouetted against what seem to be interminable skies, so Maeterlinck's protagonists are reduced in scale, shorn of the power to order their own destinies. Like an eternally mobile painting, the motifs and patterns in *Princess Maleine* circulate about in rhythmic cadences; in tendencious beats at first, then, as if activated by panic and fear, they accelerate, uncovering their paths and revealing a secret world buried in layers of anxiety.

Because of the sense of eternity implicit in the visual and textual aspects of *Princess Maleine*, it may also be considered a mystical drama. The play's action occurs in a remote northern land. Northern regions have been associated with mystical realms and the dream world. Mme de Staël stated in her volume *On Germany* that northern climes were more conducive to the imagination, that they aroused man's spiritual nature, whereas sunlit southern lands gave primacy to reason and so were looked upon by her as superficial and materialistic.

The German Romantics (Novalis, Brentano, von Arnim, Hoffmann) dug deep into their inner world — that timeless realm of essences — and transcribed their visions and insights in their works. So deeply impressed had Maeterlinck been with Novalis's *Disciples at Sais* that he later translated the book into French. Novalis had opened up the domain of the occult and of death, the realm of the mystic for Maeterlinck.

Other mystics, such as Meister Eckhart and Jakob Boehme, whose works Maeterlinck had read and admired, encouraged him to penetrate cosmic spheres: areas where feelings and sensations were no longer restricted by the phenomenological realm; where individuals who made the effort could experience the true world of reality, the eternal present, the cosmic soul and God. Eckhart had written: "There is in the soul something which is above the soul."[33] He was convinced that the spirit living in each individual, after the proper discipline, could be liberated and flow freely into the plenitude of the cosmos where both the being and his essence would become one with God.

Jakob Boehme, in his *Confessions*, wrote: "For I have seen and have known the essence of all beings, depth and nothingness."[34] He believed that within the timeless universe there existed a dynamic structure: light and darkness, good and evil, love and hate, which could be overcome via a spiritual ascension — that the Godhead could be reached and experienced with special disciplines and with God's grace, after which man would be liberated from his earthbound ways and be restored to the luminous realm of divinity.

For Maeterlinck the material, or readily visible, world was merely one aspect, a reflection of the primordial, undifferentiated unity of God's domain before creation came into existence, prior to the emergence of good and evil. Unlike Edouard Schuré, who believed that "the evils which devour men are the fruit of their choice: and that these unhappy ones seek far from them the good whose source they bear,"[35] Maeterlinck was convinced that man was virtually powerless. Man was merely a pawn in the hands of universal forces or of a higher being who imposed his will upon the world. Images, metaphors, personifications, associations, and correspondences enabled Maeterlinck to express in *Princess Maleine* his deeply pessimistic view that man is unable to order the events in his own life.

In *Princess Maleine,* a metaphysical drama, the cosmic elements come into play, imposing an aura around the protagonists and the events with which they are associated. Clouds, rain, comets, and stars ("the stars are raining") act and react upon the events depicted. Heavenly bodies are personified ("heaven is weeping over this engagement!"[36]) and play a significant role in determining the destinies of the protagonists. The heavens are depicted as black,[37] the moon as strangely red[38], all emerging from Maeterlinck's monistic world — the one living and vibrant organism of the mystic.

2. *Dramatis personae.* The *dramatis personae* are as ambiguous and as formless as Maeterlinck's spacial-time concepts. The characters are never defined; they are, rather, a series of essences reminiscent of Plato's shadows in his "Allegory of the Cave." They are like the appendages, the forces described by such mystics as the Pseudo-Dionysius, Plotinus and Ruysbroeck the Admirable; the characters are forever trying to experience the impossible: to confront destiny while aware of their powerlessness; to withdraw into themselves while hoping to make contact with others. The atmosphere in which Maeterlinck's creatures make their home is insalubrious; the *dramatis personae* are sickly. A general malaise prevails.

King Hjalmar is old, senile, and weak; his hair is falling out; he trembles while speaking and walking. "All the flames of hell are in my head!" he declares bemoaning his fate.[39] Totally dominated by Queen Anne of Jutland, his vacuous nature yields to her every desire and so he too is determined that his son, Prince Hjalmar, will marry her daughter, Uglyane.

Maeterlinck's kingly figure is antipodal to the usual monarch. Kings, generally speaking, symbolize the governing principle in man, the reasonable, virtuous and judging factors; supreme consciousness. When such wisdom wavers or becomes ill, as is the case with King Hjalmar, it indicates a negative and destructive orientation. A sick king stands for the decline or end of a prevailing society, attitude, or frame of reference, Amfortas in *Parsifal*, Shakespeare's *King Lear*, Dhritarashtra, the aged king of the Vedic epics, and Ionesco's king in *The King Must Die* are all examples of the disintegrating monarch. In these works the king has lived his life and in his old age has become a sterile force, physically and spiritually, no longer a leader, nor a maker of paths, but an instrument of decadence and destruction.

The monarchy as depicted in *Princess Maleine* is a regressive force. Such a moldy or mildewed atmosphere is comparable to the one delineated in Poe's *The Fall of the House of Usher*, with Roderick Usher's domicile sinking into the tarn. Maeterlinck's king, however, survives the ordeal, indicating that his retrogressive attitude has not yet been destroyed and that unless something drastic is accomplished, a condition of stasis may well follow.

Queen Anne, a modern version of Lady Macbeth, dominates the passive king. Ruthless, authoritarian, subtle in her conquests, desirous of power, she will stop at nothing until she achieves her end. Morality is no obstacle: she is amoral. She had already poisoned her own husband before her arrival from Jutland. It is she who murders Maleine, forcing the king to participate. Unlike Lady Macbeth, however, Queen Anne never experiences remorse; she is not overcome with anguish. She is an embodied destructive instinct, an unregenerate force.

Contrary to the fairy tale *The Sleeping Beauty*, in which an evil fairy puts the princess to sleep in some remote tower for one hundred years after which she is rescued by a prince charming, in Maeterlinck's play, Maleine's parents lock up their daughter because she refuses to renounce her prince.

Princess Maleine's parents, King Marcellus and Queen Godelive, stand for the status quo, the forces of reaction. They seek to mold their daughter so that she may "love like another," and not cause them any undue stress.[40] They are unbending and lack understanding. They represent the hard face of the law, social custom, and the fixed and regulated commerce among people.

To imprison a young girl is to symbolically stunt her psy-

chological growth, to destroy any attempt on her part to win independence, thus enabling her to evolve into womanhood. But
Maleine relies upon her own ingenuity to escape, indicating that
within her lies the strength of her convictions. She will not be
stopped. She is determined to become united with her prince at all
costs, to overcome restrictions whatever they may be.

Princess Maleine is described in a variety of ways. King Hjalmar
sees her "green face and white eyelashes!"[41] The prince views her
in a different light: "she had a way of lowering her eyes and of
crossing her hands . . . . And her gaze! — one suddenly felt as
though one were in a large canal of fresh water."[42] Her look is
strange, other protagonists remark. Maleine's coloring is white. Her
paleness lends a masklike quality to her being; like a specter
drained of blood, a dream, a phantasmagoria, an abstraction, she
meanders through the scenes.[43] Undelineated, she emerges at times
as a white cloud, "a waxen beggar,"[44] some kind of strange emanation, apparition, or astral vision comparable to the cloudy and milk-
white women depicted by Puvis de Chavannes in so many of his
canvases.

Prince Hjalmar is his father's son, passive and sickly. Indeed, he
confesses to his ill health, which is merely a replica of his psychological condition, and he remarks that the odor of dead bodies
worsens his condition.[45] "I am sick unto death and . . . I want to
rest! rest! rest!"[46] The prince is neither willing nor able to expend
the energy needed to rectify a dismal and disintegrating situation.
He knows that something within him is in a state of decay, that he is
suffering from a malaise comparable in some ways to the *mal du siè-
cle* as depicted by Chateaubriand's *René*, who lived with *ennui*, unable to rise above it. Prince Hjalmar is bathed in an atmosphere of
disenchantment and cannot assume any positive stance. Unlike the
prince charming of so many fairy tales, Prince Hjalmar is unable to
cope with his pain. He does not have the courage to cut down the
brambles that sting him and so rescue his princess. He cannot,
therefore, be identified with the solar force or with those conquerors
of old: Alexander the Great, Siegfried, St. George, and David.
These men had conquered *themselves* first, then the object of their
quest. Hjalmar is the anti-hero par excellence. Weakly constituted,
an anemic youth, he is overwhelmed by inertia, except at the very
end when he kills out of anger. The fact that he stabs the evildoer,

Queen Anne, serves no real purpose insofar as he is personally concerned. His act did destroy an evil, but only temporarily; and his own suicide did away with any possible growth on his part.

During a conversation between Uglyane (the pun in the name should be noted) and her mother, the daughter expresses her unwillingness to wear the peacock-green coat on a water-green dress. The colors don't blend, she claims.[47] Green stands for hope and fertility, which will evidently not be hers since she rejects such tonalities. Instead she gazes into her mother's mirror. There she sees "all the weeping willows in the garden,"[48] an indication that she views herself as her mother would have her be, a premonition of her unfortunate destiny. The dark forest and the clouds hiding the moon presage doom. Uglyane may be looked upon as Maleine's shadow, a being bathed in darkness, invisible since she does not stand out in her surroundings. Completely dominated by her mother, she has no identity of her own. Hjalmar is, therefore, understandably frightened of this shadow personality.

Little Allan is one of the many children appearing in Maeterlinck's dramas. He represents budding, the emergence of newborn ideas. He has not yet been destroyed by his mother. Loved by those surrounding him, he relates best to Maleine whom he calls "his mother."[49] He is haunted with fear at the thought that Maleine may disappear or that she may get sick. "She will no longer play with me?"[50] he cries. His concern increases as the play goes on. Queen Anne does not take his anguish seriously. She distracts him and tells him to play with his ball. The child, however, remains undaunted, unwilling to accept the pat answers offered him. Still in touch with nature, he experiences the atmosphere of death viscerally long before the act has been perpetrated, and for this reason knows the true meaning of terror.

3. *Symbols.* The symbols, the most important of which are the tower, forest, water, sun, moon, and castle, may be considered protagonists in *Princess Maleine*. They compel certain vital forces into activity. Their power rests on a whole network of associations that affect all aspects of the drama and those who view it.

A propensity for heights as exemplified in the tower image indicates a need for ascension, a desire for higher realms, thus permitting a wide view into the distance. However, danger awaits those at-

tracted to overly high domains, as attested to in the Tower of Babel
allegory in the Bible. With a poor view of the earth (or workaday
reality), confusion in the rational sphere may ensue. Heights encourage a sense of isolation and may act as a compensatory force for
those who are unable to relate to others in existential matters.
Maleine, however, breaks out of her tower, thus demonstrating her
need to come to grips with earthly content. It is significant that
Maleine's tower has no window and no doors so that she is unable to
see either sun or moon.[51] Deprived of sight and far above the
terrestrial sphere, she might have remained entombed, disoriented,
and cut off. In medieval tales, the *Lais* of Marie de France, young
brides were frequently imprisoned in towers until they either struck
out for themselves or were rescued by some good force. The Nurse
in Maeterlinck's drama tries to convince Maleine to obey her
parents, to be passive: "Was it so difficult to submit outwardly, and
to renounce that weeping willow of a Hjalmar who wouldn't even
budge his little finger to deliver us?"[52] She encourages Maleine to
take the easy way out, to conform, to yield to the wishes of the
status quo. The Nurse's attitude as well as the views of Maleine's
parents, are symbolized by the tower atmosphere: the tower is not
only virtually hermetically sealed, it also crawls with fungi and bats,
all examples of decay and regression. But Maleine refuses to submit.
Like Anouilh's Antigone, she is determined to follow her own inclinations.

When Prince Hjalmar sees the tower from a distance, he says it
resembles a windmill, perhaps reminiscent of Don Quixote's illusions. As he approaches the structure, he notices the name of
Queen Anne inscribed on a stone. The tower, at this juncture, has a
dual meaning: an inner subtle value in that his beloved Maleine is
imprisoned there and an outer value that stands for Queen Anne's
world. If he projects a dual image onto the tower, he may be looked
upon as a man divided — the inner man, associated with Maleine, a
soul figure; and the outer man, likened to the exterior world and the
forces of destruction as represented by Queen Anne. Both attitudes
live within him in an unconscious state, both are experienced
passively.

The forest in which Hjalmar and Maleine find themselves at
various intervals in the drama figures frequently in fairy tales. It il-
lustrates a dark, archaic, primeval realm where chaos usually reigns.

The nettles, brambles, and confusion inherent in such an atmosphere are usually brought to order by a hero's or heroine's determined action. In *Princess Maleine* the forest is reminiscent of an underworld domain, the unconscious. If they were to remain in the forest, Hjalmar and Maleine would become victims of their fantasies.[53] When Maleine is alone in the forest, she comments on its blackness, on her inability to see clearly and on the wolves and wild boars inhabiting it. Later, Maleine and her Nurse remain in the forest for twelve hours. They lose their way, meet some strangers, and finally see her parents' castle burn down. "Everyone is dead in the country over there,"[54] Maleine says. She has, so to speak, burned her bridges behind her. For Maleine the forest was a productive force. It was in the forest, seeing her parents' castle aflame in the distance, that she came to know her independent spirit. In breaking with her past, she was no longer dominated by it.

A distinction must be made between the thick forest and the woods in the park surrounding Hjalmar's castle. A park or garden usually indicates an Eden-like atmosphere, an ordered world, "the paradisiacal childhood realm, an enclosed area radiating calm." Hjalmar does not see the park in this light. He looks upon it as a cemetery. "I have gravedigger's hands," he claims, as though boding evil, "It's strange here tonight."[55] Hjalmar thinks Uglyane is entering the park when in reality it is Maleine. "We will see each other in the clarity of the water," he tells her.[56] Maleine is fearful. How will he react when he discovers her identity, she wonders. Hjalmar insists she come closer, that she walk into the light. "You are strange tonight! It's as though my eyes had opened tonight. — It's as though my heart had partially opened tonight . . . . It seems that I never really looked at you until now!"[57] He sees her as beautiful. Insight has come to him finally — in the darkness.

Water images are replete in the drama: tears, fountains, weeping willows. "We will see each other in the clarity of the water";[58] "The fountain, agitated by the wind, is bending and falls on them again";[59] "Someone is crying here"; "The fountain is sobbing strangely and is dying".[60] Water is formless; it is in a perpetual state of flux. It represents frequently a world *in potentia* before form or rigidity have come into being. A fluid body may be considered a dynamic and motivating force. It has been linked with the mother image, a nourishing agent, for without water nothing can exist. To be immersed in water is to be renewed, regenerated, and reborn, as symbolized by the ceremony of baptism. But water also has negative attributes. One may drown in water, like Narcissus. In *Princess Maleine* water represents the utterly formless protagonists who weave their way in and out of the events, as trickling water is compelled by some outer force.

The sun is also a significant image. A tiny beam of sunlight shines through the cracks in the tower, which is otherwise dark. "There is some [sun] on my dress. Some on my hands!"[61] cries Maleine in utter joy. This fecund force indicates the beginnings of life. Solar energy is at work. Maleine looks out from the crevice and sees a ship at sea with white sails. She is imbued with a sense of freedom, which encourages and strengthens her to seek her way. Her feelings of happiness are expressed in a series of refrains reminiscent of ancient medieval rounds: she enumerates the various objects that come into view: the city, the belfry, the sea, roads, prairies. The repetitions in her song have a hypnotic effect on her and lull her into a dream world where fantasy and pleasure become distinct possibilities.

In the lunar sequences, and most frequently in the forest scenes, a sense of turmoil, of foreboding is ushered in. When there is an interplay of light and dark — as if sun and moon were in conflict — panic is injected into the picture.[62] When, for example, Maleine is about to die, her large black dog, Pluto, begins to tremble in the corner.[63] His blackness stands out in sharp contrast with Maleine's lunar or white vestments. "My light was extinguished when I opened the door,"[64] the Nurse says. It is in this blackened atmosphere, after both sun and moon have withdrawn, that Hjalmar discovers Maleine — dead.

Princess Maleine introduces spectators to the domain of Thanatos. "One more night like this one and we will all be white!" mirrors the negative attitude in this drama. Nothing beneficial emerges from the destructive outcome in the play. There is no spirit of self-sacrifice, no ascension of spiritual values, no lesson to be drawn from the suffering of the protagonists. Dark forces have taken precedence. Chaos reigns.

Maeterlinck sent a copy of *Princess Maleine* to Mallarmé in Paris, who gave it to Paul Hervieu, who in turn sent it to Octave Mirbeau for possible review in the *Figaro*. Several months passed without news. Then, one Sunday, when Maeterlinck was dining in the country with his family, the valet entered with the day's mail.[65] Among the letters was a copy of the *Figaro*, with the following review:

I know nothing about Maurice Maeterlinck . . . . I only know that no one is less known than he, and I know only that he has written a masterpiece, not the kind of masterpiece published daily by our young masters . . . but an admirable and pure and eternal masterpiece, a masterpiece which can immortalize a name . . . a masterpiece which honest and tormented artists have dreamt of writing in their hours of enthusiasm, and as no one until now has written. Finally, M. Maurice Maeterlinck has given us the most original work of this time and the most extraordinary and the most naïve also, comparable, do I dare say it? superior in beauty to what is most beautiful in Shakespeare? This work is entitled "Princess Maleine."[66]

Maeterlinck was dumbfounded and overwhelmed by Mirbeau's critique. He wrote to him in his typically modest manner.

You were wrong in considering me a great poet, I am merely a groping child . . . . I only see the influence of Shakespeare, Poe, and that of my friend Van Lerberghe in my poor Princess. I distinguish nothing else which belongs to me.[67]

Mirbeau's criticism did much to increase Maeterlinck's faith in himself and everyone seemed to want to read *Princess Maleine*. Fifty copies of the original edition were available when the review came out, and all of these were sold. But by the time the publisher brought out the second edition, enthusiasm had waned, and there was little financial remuneration with *Princess Maleine*. Psychologically, however, it had been a catalyst.

CHAPTER 2

The Death Dramas

I   The Intruder — A Rite de Passage

M AETERLINCK'S first "critical" success encouraged him to rent a small apartment in Brussels. There he lived in relative calm. No financial worries plagued him since he accepted support from his parents. Almost immediately, therefore, he set to work on his second play, *L'Intruse* ("The Intruder"), first called *The Approach*.

The Intruder is a play about death. A family, consisting of a blind Grandfather, an Uncle, a Father, and three girls, awaits the Mother's recovery after childbirth. A relative is expected. The Father and Uncle are convinced the Mother is out of danger. Only the blind Grandfather senses the hopelessness of the situation. The visitor finally arrives — in the form of Death.

The play was first produced on May 20, 1891, in Paris at Paul Fort's Théâtre d'Art. Fort, only eighteen years of age, had founded his theater the previous year when still a student at the Lycée Louis le Grand.

The program, which included Maeterlinck's *The Intruder*, had been planned as a benefit for Verlaine and Gauguin. It was decided that *The Intruder* would be placed at the end of the program so that if the evening proved to be too lengthy, it could be withdrawn. However, the poetry recitations and short sketches that preceded the play did not preclude its performance.

The Intruder is constructed almost exclusively of the exteriorization of inner states. The actors, almost immobile throughout the performance, have pared their gestures down to the barest nuances of movement, underscoring by their very restraint the mounting terror of the situation. The dialogue is sparse. Words are enunciated with objectivity and yet with infinite tonal and rhythmic variations.

They sometimes sound metallic; at other moments they take on the solemnity of a religious chant. The actors, including Lugné-Poë, later to be director of the Théâtre de l'Oeuvre, played with a minimum of gestures.

Nor is the visual aspect of *The Intruder* neglected. The troubled characters grouped together on stage hide behind masks in the excruciating anxieties that corrode their lives. The glazed eyes of one, the enigmatic smile of the second, the deeply furrowed brow of the third are reminiscent of the canvases of certain Flemish primitives: Dirk Bouts and Roger Van der Weyden. They succeed in concretizing sensation, stifling feelings, and imposing the stamp of eternity on their works. Divested of personal elements, the characters in *The Intruder* are mythlike, mediumistic. They flay each other on stage in the subtlest of ways, compelled to do so, seemingly, by some invisible network of fatal forces.

Philosophically *The Intruder* is based on a series of vague or strange encounters, representing man's confrontation with occult forces over which he has no control. Maeterlinck, let us recall, had been deeply influenced by the Symbolist poets — Baudelaire, Mallarmé, Villiers de l'Isle Adam. The Symbolists as well as Maeterlinck rebelled most dramatically against positivism, as exhibited by Auguste Comte and Hippolyte Taine, who believed in applying to philosophy and religion the same system of observation that scientists used. In his *Course on Philosophical Positivism* Comte berated all those who accepted as factual or real anything that could not be proven by scientific method. Influenced by both Hegel and Comte, Taine also fostered belief in scientific determinism. He considered free will to be nearly ineffectual in altering human destinies; heredity and environmental factors alone were determining. Taine's theory based on race, milieu, and moment became the creed for the Naturalist writers. Emile Zola based a series of novels on Taine's theories.

Maeterlinck rejected the ultrascientific and experimental spirit of his age. He sought to divest art of the crude and obvious realities so blatantly included in the writings of the Naturalists. He refused to dramatize the vicissitudes of the lives of alcoholics, prostitutes, syphilitics, and impoverished suffering human beings. Such endeavors were the concern of the Naturalist director André Antoine, the founder of the Théâtre Libre (1887). Antoine believed in the "slice of life," or "peephole," theatre. He viewed the stage as a sort of laboratory where scientific investigations were carried out. There was no *trompe l'oeil* scenery in the plays produced at the Théâtre Libre. If the drama took place in a butcher shop, real pieces of meat were placed on stage.

Just as repugnant to Maeterlinck as the Naturalist credo were the obvious and cheap extravaganzas produced at the boulevard theaters in Paris. The goal of these directors was money; little attention was paid to esthetics. Nor did the government-subsidized Comédie-Française with its star-studded system (Sarah Bernhardt, Mounet-Sully, de Max, the Coquelins) appeal to Maeterlinck. He felt that the play as a totality was unimportant to these so-called *monstres sacrés*. Only their personal performance and the aggrandizement of their ego counted. But for Maeterlinck theater reflected an inner search based on an intuitive experience. He sought to create a mood and to make man's soul manifest through a silent stage language and through rituals devoid of nearly all motion, each restrained gesture being a sign or symbol suggesting some profound and mysterious reality. A nearly static condition had to reign on stage, permitting, Maeterlinck believed, the intrusion of occult forces into the dramatic happenings, and thereby creating an atmosphere weighted with tension as each of the protagonists slowly became acquainted with his *karma*.

Profoundly influenced by Emerson's *Essays* and by the writings of the Flemish mystic Jan van Ruysbroeck the Admirable, whose *The Adornment of the Spiritual Marriage* he translated, Maeterlinck looked upon the world not via his intellect, but through his senses. He followed the dictates of his heart and feelings, enabling him to experience nature in its dual aspects as Nourisher and Destroyer. He understood and attempted to accept these forces that serve both to link and sever man from the universal flow. "There is a correspondence between the human soul and everything that exists in the world; more properly, everything that is known to man," Emerson wrote in his *Diary*. "Instead of studying things without, the principles of them all may be penetrated into within him." Maeterlinck's search, therefore, was turned inward. Ruysbroeck stressed the unity of existence: the light-drenched realm of God as well as the darkened sphere of matter, the latter also imbued with the divine essence, but to a lesser degree than the former. Frequently Ruybsbroeck walked from the fields surrounding the hermitage of Groenendael to the forest of Soignes near Brussels. There, in the serene stillness of nature, he meditated until he felt God's powerful force flow into him.

And in consequence of this enlightened [feeling] men have found within themselves an essential contemplation which is above reason and without reason, and a fruitive tendency which pierces through every condition and all being, and through which they immerse themselves in a wayless abyss of fathomless beatitude.[1]

Technically speaking, *The Intruder* is a modern piece, simple and poignant. The fact that *The Intruder* adheres to the French classical unities of time, place, and action is an indication of its conciseness and depth. There is no extraneous action, nothing superfluous. Everything on stage emerges directly from the body of the text. Action and playing time are the same: one and a half hours. The set does not change. It consists of a room with three doors and a window, the window opening onto a garden. The door to the left leads to the dying woman's room; the one to the right to the infant's room; the third, back center stage, leads to the outside world. The doors may be looked upon as three aspects of existence: death, life, and chance. Hovering over this ultrastationary and lugubrious atmosphere of doom are, as Maeterlinck writes in his preface to the 1929 edition of his Théâtre, "enormous invisible and fatal powers."

The protagonists in *The Intruder* should not be looked upon as flesh-and-blood beings, rather as archetypes — primordial images arising from the profoundest layers of man's unconscious. The fact that the blind Grandfather is the only one to sense his daughter's imminent death may be regarded today as a theatrical cliché. However, if examined in the light of the latest scientific and psychological knowledge, he becomes a *nouveauté*. His outlook upon the world is termed *synchronistic* or *acausal*. Because the Grandfather has been exiled from the visible world, cut off symbolically from the realm of Ideas (or the rational principle in man), he finds solace in a world of senses and feeling. He, therefore, experiences life on a different level than do the Uncle, the Father, and the girls.

The Grandfather's intuitions and premonitory statements throughout the play rest on an inner illumination, made fruitful in a realm where the limited linear time and space factors of rational man have been transcended. The Grandfather exists in a dimensionless universe, and for this reason some of his statements may appear at first contradictory. A blind man would not say about his daughter, when evidence points to the contrary, "I believe she is not very well . . .[2] something has happened. . . .[3] I am certain my daughter is worse! . . . But you people don't see clearly. . . ."[4] Like a plant that draws sustenance from the darkness of the earth, the Grandfather gains his powers from the mysterious realm of sightlessness. Only he understands the meaning of the fourth dimension. That is, he alone has the ability to live beyond the physical space-time delineations. Because the Grandfather lives almost exclusively in his inner world (his unconscious), he no longer responds exclusively to the temporal divisions imposed upon rational man in his attempt to order his existential habits. Although the Grandfather's conversations sometimes seem to relate directly to the dialogue of the other protagonists, actually their import reaches far beyond their superficial vision. He senses the tremendous weight of doom and the presence of the Intruder because it is already there. Its spirit merely imposes itself more acutely upon him as the drama unfolds.

Ever since Newton established his theory of causality, man has been led to believe that everything within the universe has a causal explanation. If Newton's law were valid, then it might be postulated that chance itself is the result of a causality that has not yet come into existence. How is such a concept possible? How could certain telepathic, synchronistic, or acausal experiences occur in a causal universe? Swedenborg, for example, when living in London, had a vision of his native city Stockholm in flames at the very moment the fire was raging. The thought and the event had occurred simultaneously regardless of spatial distances. An acausal event is difficult to comprehend, yet actually does exist. Today's physicists have not yet determined the reasons for such events but are studying the phenomenon.

How do such sensations become manifest to the Grandfather? By means of what C. G. Jung calls archetypal patterns, which he defines as those contents or forces that exist in the deepest strata of man's being. Under certain circumstances, archetypes emerge from the unconscious in the form of images which, when interpreted, may be helpful in determining the situation at hand. As archetypes flow into consciousness, they are accompanied by certain affects (feelings, moods, sensations) that may not always be explicated along rational lines. The Grandfather in *The Intruder* experiences these affects in terms of impulses, intuitions, and perceptions. As these unconscious contents emerge, they frequently have no rational or causal relationship with the objective situation as far as the other protagonists in the play are concerned. The Grandfather therefore is at times, ironically enough, the subject of mockery. He is a being who lives on the edge of two worlds and for this reason understands the meaning of the messages emanating from his spaceless and timeless universe.

To reinforce the dichotomy between the Grandfather's approach to life and the superficial attitudes revealed by the rest of the family's conversation, Maeterlinck had recourse to certain theatrical vehicles based on sound, sensation, and images. These were designed to intrude upon the restrained and static atmosphere of the drama. The varying reactions of the protagonists to these devices served to heighten the atmosphere of growing terror, fear, and mystery. Because the dialogue was so Spartan and the action so bone hard, any change of pace, imagery, or rhythmic interchange was certain to arouse visceral reactions on the part of the spectator, shaking him frequently into a new frame of awareness — alienating him, in the Brechtian sense, only to reach him more deeply seconds later.

The antique Flemish standing clock in a corner of the stage may be considered as a vehicle intended to jar the atmosphere every now and then. The clock rings out the hour and half hour during the play — from 11 o'clock until midnight — up to the advent of death. The clock represents a linear frame of reference. It underscores the irreversible and destructive nature of time, man's victimization by this force, the fragility and ephemeral nature of his life. The finality of the rings, which fall like hatchet sounds, and the protracted silences between the clangs are reminiscent of certain medieval French chants depicting the march of the hours during Christ's agony on the cross. For the Grandfather, who already knows his daughter's death is imminent, the chiming of the clock merely confirms his feelings, and so his reactions to the noise are disconnected. "Am I turned toward the glass door?"[5] he questions after hearing the sound. He awaits the fulfillment of destiny. The others in the room, because they live in a linear dimension, concentrate increasingly on the passage of time.

The sounds of birds and the wind rustling in the trees in the garden may be considered another kind of audible invasion from the existential world. The Father has asked one of his daughters to look out of the window to see if the relative they are expecting is coming down the garden path. The girl sees no one. Instead she hears the nightingales singing and the wind blowing. Suddenly and for no apparent reason, there is silence.[6]

Ancient Egyptians worshiped a bird deity with a human head. In their hieroglyphics, this theriomorphic deity represented the Ba, the soul, implying that the bird being a volatile and active force, was the bearer of the soul to astral planes. In *The Intruder* the fact that the singing birds stop abruptly would indicate the gravity of the occasion, the hushed silence at the soul's passing. According to Buddhist doctrine, wind has been associated with Buddha's breath; Hebrew tradition (*ruh* means both "breath" and "spirit" in Hebrew) likens it to the "creative breath" as exemplified in Genesis when God "breathed in his [Adam's] nostrils the breath of life; and man became a living soul." (2:7) When wind or breath ceases, life has been withdrawn.

Other intrusions serve to jar the condition of stasis on stage. The gardener, for example, who is sharpening his scythe outside, causes the Grandfather to shudder.[7] The other protagonists react to this noise in a normal manner, as part of the natural occurrence. The scythe, associated with Saturn, the god of time (irreversible and destructive), may be considered a symbol of death. Because the scythe is curved, it takes on lunar (passive, nocturnal) characteristics, or female attributes, and may therefore be linked to the fate of the dying mother in the play. Because the Grandfather alone knows the portent of this noise, he reacts dramatically to the grating sound. He becomes tense, for he believes the sharpening of the scythe is taking place within the house and not outside, as the others claim.

The sound of footsteps also intensifies the atmosphere of foreboding. The Grandfather hears not one but two sets of footsteps downstairs: those of the servant and those of the visitor. The other protagonists are uncertain but tend to believe that only the servant's are audible. A door is heard to shut downstairs. The tension mounts by degrees as the footsteps grow louder. The anxiety becomes almost unbearable as the door opens and the servant enters. The Grandfather is convinced that the visitor is accompanying the servant. "Is she crying?" he asks. "Of course not," the Uncle replies, wondering why the Grandfather should ask such a question.[8] The servant is interrogated. Has anyone entered the house? No one, she assures them. Why, then, did she shut the door downstairs? Because it was open. "But who opened it?" the Father questions. No one knows the reply. "You brought someone into the room," the Grandfather asserts, almost accusing the others of deceit.[9]

As the play draws to a finale, the clock tolls midnight. The anguished wail of the infant in the room to the right is heard. "The wail continues with gradations of terror." Hurried footsteps are heard from the room to the left, then silence. The protagonists listen in mute terror. The door to the left opens. The Sister of Charity appears on the threshhold. She makes the sign of the cross and announces the Mother's death. The Intruder — death — has indeed arrived, as the Grandfather had predicted.[10]

Sensations are also used as a device to render all the more acute the fright conveyed in *The Intruder*. The Grandfather complains of a growing malaise, a sense of claustrophobia, He asks for the window to be opened. Moments later, however, he requests that the window be shut — "It seems that the cold has entered the room." According to Pythagoreans, cold is synonymous with death. Fire or bodily heat is associated with the flame of life or health. Heraclitus too believed that fire (heat) was an "agent of transformation" since everything is born from fire and returns to it, like the phoenix that is destroyed and is regenerated from its own ashes. The Grandfather is experiencing the chill of death vicariously. He feels life ebbing from his daughter's body.

The sensations of heat and fire are conveyed from a visual point of view as well, by means of the interplay of light and darkness inside and outside the room. On stage the candle burns brightly; and because of the shadows it casts, so reminiscent of the paintings of Georges de la Tour, the life-and-death drama becomes increasingly palpable. Despite the light, however, the Grandfather declares: "It seems to me that there isn't much light here,"[11] indicating a lack of comprehension, an illusory optimism, on the part of the other family members. As the play progresses, the Father notices a dimming of the light. "The lamp is not burning well tonight."[12] The Grandfather then asks if the lamp has been extinguished because he no longer feels the light and believes himself to be more cut off from the others than ever. "I am here, all alone, in endless darkness!" Ironically, he comments on the "pallor" of the three girls: "I feel that you are all paler than the dead!"[13] The lamp is then personified: it "palpitates," it acts "concerned," the "cold wind is tormenting it." When the lamp finally goes out and the family sits in darkness, each taking on the appearance of the shadow of death, one realizes that the various gradations of the flame were a material manifestation of an inner happening.

The moonlight in the garden also mirrors the course of the Intruder's march. The daughter looking out of the window has seen an avenue of cypress trees in the light of the moon.[14] The moon, always associated with woman because of its periodic phases and curved contours, indicates in this instance the Mother's fate. As the moon pales, hiding behind clouds and finally fading out of sight — in rhythm with the flickering candle — it becomes a sign that death and the Mother are united.

The color green, visible through the window, represents worldly productivity and fertility. The dark, drab, brownish tinctures predominating within the room spell death and decay. Both worlds are visible from the orchestra — implying that life and death are merely aspects of a totality. The Grandfather represents such a totality for he experiences both simultaneously.

The Intruder is a play of cosmic dimension, a work that dramatizes a supreme interchange: the Mother, stage left, who is about to exit from life, and the infant, stage right, who is entering the earthly domain. It is a scenic depiction of life's cyclical orbit, what is termed in myths and religions a *rite de passage*.

Artaud called Maeterlinck's dramas a series of "encounters," which, personal and subjective at the outset, are of such vast dimension that they have embedded themselves into the collective sphere, that of the work of art.

The Intruder was one of the most successful dramas produced at Paul Fort's Théâtre d'Art. The critics were virtually unanimous in their praise. The usually difficult Francisque Sarçey of the *Temps* was enormously impressed by Maeterlinck's originality and the intensity of a drama based on the waiting principle (*drame d'attente*), silences, and a sense of doom. Henry Bauer of the *Echo de Paris* noted the "scenic power" of Maeterlinck's play, which had left him with "an extroardinary impression of pathos . . . . The work is one of the most breathtaking ever, and nowhere that I know of has the impression of the reality of immaterial sensations been rendered with such intensity, in such a concrete form. Maurice Maeterlinck's act is of a powerful and sensitive art . . . it's a new form, profoundly moving in its depiction of human tragedy in the theatre."[15]

II The Blind — *The Dying Complex*

Maeterlinck's drama *Les Aveugles* ("The Blind") was staged on December 11, 1891, at Paul Fort's Théâtre d'Art, seven months after his first success. Laforgue's *The Fairylike Council* and *The Song of Songs* were included in the program. During the latter dramatization, perfume was sprayed throughout the theatre to create in true symbolic manner (or so they believed) what Baudelaire had called *correspondences* — that is, the unification of the senses: sight, smell, touch, and feeling. Such antics did not serve the dramatists' cause, but rather promoted laughter among the audience. To go to such lengths to create an atmosphere of mystery and mysticism seemed artificial, even ridiculous.

Despite some negative criticism by Julien Leclercq of the *Mercure de France* (January 1892), who believed *The Blind* was too static a piece, the play was well received by the Symbolists Mirbeau, Mallarmé, and their coterie.

Perhaps more important than this enthusiasm was the fact that after the performances of *The Blind*, Maeterlinck and Lugné-Poë became close friends, the theatrical director becoming instrumental in the dramatist's evolution.[16]

The play itself is of metaphysical dimension. It is essentially the dramatization of what psychologists have labeled the "dying complex." That an eschatological situation should be the focal point of a creative work indicates an attempt on the part of the author to come to terms with the notion of death on a conscious level. To experience death unconsciously is to be unequipped to differentiate between subject and object. Under these circumstances the subject identifies with the world around him: the family, environment, nation. No individual identity can come into being; no ego growth is thus possible. However, once differentiation does occur, as it does progressively in *The Blind*, a sense of isolation, loneliness, and fear makes its appearance. Illustrations of fright are prevalent in myths (Siegfried) and fairy tales ("The Boy Who Learned to Shudder"), in which young men travel far from home and go through a series of harrowing experiences, learning thus to cope with the dangers of life and becoming aware of their own limitations. An encounter with fear is a necessity if a cleavage between subject and object is to take place, and with it an emergence from an infantile Garden of Eden atmosphere. Genesis teaches us that birth and death came into existence with Cain and Abel. Opposition, conflict, and antagonism followed — dynamic forces that are essential to the learning and maturation process. Consequently, man became aware of the fact that death belongs to life and vice versa, that these polarities form a totality — implicit in the cosmos' cyclical plan.

The dying complex dramatized in Maurice Maeterlinck's *The Blind* may be likened in theme to Samuel Beckett's *Waiting for Godot* or *End Game*. Both dramatists experienced a profound sense of metaphysical despair and futility, a concern for linear time (the years allotted to man on earth) as opposed to cyclical or eternal (cosmic) time. They felt a desperate need to hope (symbolized at times by the child image), to wait for some illusory salvation to earthly anguish, and, paradoxically, the desire to put a stop to new beginnings, thereby ending man's cycle of birth, life, and death; a determination on the part of finite beings to struggle in order to understand the infinite universe.

The Blind has no real plot. Its strength lies in its concise language, economy of motility, and emotional restraint. Whatever action may be inherent in the drama has already taken place before the curtain rises. Suspense consists in waiting.

Twelve blind people from the home for the blind have been led into the forest by their leader-priest. He had wanted them to become acquainted with the mountains and the sea surrounding the island on which they live to broaden, so to speak, their knowledge of the world. He tells the people to wait for him while he investigates their whereabouts. And there they remain: six blind men seated on stone slabs opposite six blind women, three of whom pray throughout the performance; one, a young "crazy girl," holds a baby on her lap. The audience, however, sees (back center stage) the old priest, dressed in a thick black coat and hat, leaning against a large cavernous tree trunk. He is dead. The drama consists in the growing anxiety of the twelve as they await the priest's return, their terror and feelings of abandonment when they discover their leader's death, and their plea at the end for "pity" as they face eventual death from cold and hunger.

For Maeterlinck the sightless protagonists represent those who have been exiled from the Godhead, the Garden of Eden, souls thrust into the material world, fallen into evil, becoming human beings. They grope about in the forest, limited in their capacities, vainly attempting to find their way back to the safety and security of their institution — that is, conventional attitudes and frames of reference.

The blind are, psychologically speaking, living out a *shadow* existence, not able to experience life in terms of themselves as individuals. They are followers of their priest-guide. The priest has certain Christlike attributes: he is a self-sacrificing figure who had tried to help the blind throughout their years in the home, by instructing and protecting them. As long as they followed his dictates and lived within the security of the institution ("within the shelter of the walls"), they felt comforted because "there is nothing to fear when the door is shut."

A way of life germinated within the home for the blind. The validity of the resulting ideations, however, could be tested only by a confrontation with the outside world — the "open door." Growth is a dynamic process that needs conflict and activity. Binary opposition is obligatory if existence is to be experienced fully. If introversion dominates for too long a period — as symbolized by the life spent in the institution — a condition of stasis, which is antithetical to life, occurs. The blind, therefore, had to leave their institution and make their way into the outside world; they had to experience the terror of isolation, to live in a world of opposition in order to understand the significance of their own lives.

Like Boehme, Swedenborg, Plotinus, and other Neoplatonists, Maeterlinck believed that it is man's obligation to ascend the spiritual ladder: from sightlessness to illumination, from the constriction of the soul to its liberation. Although man, during his earthly sojourn, is part of the finite realm, he is also an outgrowth of the infinite world and hence is endowed with both mortal and immortal characteristics. Certain humans are provided, Maeterlinck suggested, with the ability to see beyond the rational or intellectual sphere of reference and *know* more than others. Moreover, man is not born equal. Maeterlinck makes his position quite clear when describing his characters: some were born blind and others were deprived of their sight later in life. Variations, gradations, and hierarchies are thus established within the group. A sameness pervades on the outside, nevertheless, in that all are blind, none is given a proper name.

The dichotomy established in *The Blind* in terms of the years of sightlessness experienced by the protagonists may be likened to the infinite gradations inherent in society and to each being's capacity to fulfill his potential. Maeterlinck believed, as had Emerson, whose influence upon him was primordial, that the poet (the creative individual) was a superior being, a "representative" man, and that his wisdom must be recognized by humanity.

The poet, for Maeterlinck, was like the Roman *vates*. He is endowed with "the largest power to receive and to impart profound truths. . ."; he is intuitive, inspired, and imaginative; through his art he gives form to the realities experienced in his unconscious and to the spiritual forces discovered within his depths.

Emerson had selected Plato, Swedenborg, and Shakespeare, to list but a few, as worthy of his admiration, as "great men" who are "the lenses through which we read our minds." In "The Over-Soul" Emerson described the poet's power:

. . .a great public power on which he can draw, by unlocking, at all risks, his human doors, and suffering the ethereal tides to roll and circulate through him; then he is caught up into the life of the Universe, his speech is thunder, his thought is law, and his works are as universally intelligible as the plants and animals.

Even the poet is blind; in that he is flesh and blood, embedded in the material world, his ways are circumscribed. Because forces beyond his control shape his destiny, he is not always permitted to act according to the dictates of his will. Consistent with Schopenhauerian dicta, Maeterlinck's protagonists are deceived into believing themselves masters of their own fate. At first they are convinced their leader-priest will protect them from all dangers and they will eventually be led to safety. Only as the drama progresses are they confronted with realities: the priest's death and their own isolation and deprivation of free will. At the end of the play, they are finally made aware of their fate and limitations.

Maeterlinck was indeed a nineteenth-century man. He had been brought up to believe in progress and in man's eventual conquest over nature through science and rational thinking. The years spent at the Jesuit College of Sainte-Barbe had taught him to believe in St. Augustine's concept of a uniquely good God and that evil has no substance and reality and is merely a *privatio boni*. Maeterlinck's belief eventually became incompatible with the realities of life. Unlike men such as Paul Claudel, Charles Péguy, and François Mauriac, whose faith in the tenets of Catholicism gave them a *raison d'être* and filled them with energy and hope, Maeterlinck was divested of his beliefs and sunk into a state of despair and apathy. His personal suffering was brought to a climax when he began his confrontation with life. *The Blind* is the fruit of his solitude and meditations, and as such is a symbolic representation of his psychological growth. To a great extent, *The Blind* represents a parallel drama occuring in Maeterlinck's unconscious.

It is significant that the play takes place in a forest. In *Princess Maleine* forest imagery was only intermittent. A primeval association is inherent in the forest symbol, particularly as described in Maeterlinck's stage directions: a forest "with an eternal aspect beneath a profoundly starry sky." One has the distinct impression that the forest symbolizes a sinking into some past or collective unconscious. It is within this deepest of arcane realms that there occurs a reshuffling of feelings, notions, and sensations which are exteriorized via archetypal images. To understand the full import of *The Blind*, therefore, as well as certain aspects of Maeterlinck's personal psychology, the visualizations set forth in the drama must be analyzed.

The forest, the institution of the blind, and the island on which they are indicate, each in its own manner, a sort of exile — a cutting off from the mainstream of life. Such images usher in feelings of isolation and solitude that are in themselves ambivalent. They indicate a need to sever relations with the outside world and to exteriorize energies that would otherwise be diffused into coping with external problems. Inner growth may, under such circumstances, take place. The images also can act as an escape mechanism or a protective barrier against collective misunderstanding and rejection.

Interestingly enough, Maeterlinck was experiencing a rebellious attitude against intrusions on his personal life. In a letter to a friend (October 4, 1890), a little more than a year prior to the production of *The Blind*, he wrote:

I beg you *in all sincerity, in all sincerity,* to prevent, if you can, the interviews you mention, for God's sake prevent them from taking place. I am beginning to be terribly tired of all this. Yesterday, while I was dining, two reporters from [names of newspapers] just dropped in on me. I am going to leave for London because I am sick about what's happening to me. So, if you can't turn the interviewers away, they will end up by interviewing my domestic.[18]

Maeterlinck was adamant. He sought desperately to continue his contemplative existence. He was determined; nothing would interfere with it. Evidently he needed this period of retrenchment to *indwell.* It was imperative for him to experience that terrible "darkness of the mind," that "suffering of the soul" psychologists have labeled "melancholia" and St. John of the Cross calls "the dark night of the soul." During such periods individuals are gripped by the chthonic powers living within their own unconscious and must come to terms with them for survival and growth. *The Blind* is Maeterlinck's "night sea journey."

The protagonists number twelve. Like Christ's disciples, they follow their master, the priest. According to numerology, twelve represents cosmic order. In that this number has been associated with the twelve signs of the zodiac and certain mathematical equations connected with time and space, it is considered a complete, or whole, number. Inertia consequently may take hold. St. Matthew (28:10) tells us that Christ's disciples went out into the highways to "teach all nations," but such activity took place only after the twelve had been reduced to eleven following Judas' betrayal and suicide. The addition or deletion of a number (11, 13) destroyed the whole (12), created an odd number, an irritant, thereby causing a dynamic process to set in. According to the mystic

Eliphas Lévi, "Thirteen is the number of death and birth. . . of war and of treaties."[19] The twelve in *The Blind* became thirteen when the baby made its presence known by beginning to cry at the end of the drama. The counterforce or irritant needed to set up a kinetic situation that could lead to growth and self-consciousness took the form of the baby, a symbol of hope (as it had in religious ideations: baby Horus, baby Dionysus, baby Moses, baby Jesus, and so on. Ironically it is the crazy woman whose infant figures in the play, implying that one must be irrational to seek to continue the wheel of life and to yield to one's *karma*.

The fact that the old priest, the leader of the blind, has died, is of great significance. The priest is a patriarchal figure, a spiritual guide, a mediator between God and man, a representative of the church, of order, and of conventional ideology. He stands for the patriarchal, or *senex* God of occidental culture, the one to whom man prays, "Our father who art in Heaven."[20] The priest leads the blind into the highways and byways of life symbolically but dies in the endeavor. The blind, seemingly, could become conscious individuals only after their leader's death, the Father or Christ figure had to be removed.

As a patriarchal figure, the priest encompassed both positive and negative forces: positive in that he had always protected his followers and thus was a containing factor, a representative of secure and tried ways; negative in that he had himself begun to question his ideations, had thrust his "sheep" into the world of chance and danger, then abandoned them (against his will) to the forest. The priest, therefore, is a composite primal father, like Odin and Shiva (both creators and destroyers). He stands for good and evil, security and danger, life and death. He resembles not the all-good God of St. Augustine, but rather the "total" God of the mystic: of Jakob Boehme, Ruysbroeck the Admirable, the Hebrew God of the Bible, and the Kabbala.

The senex figure — the priest in *The Blind* — usually appears in creative works, myths, and fairy tales when advice or insight is needed or when existentialist attitudes have led to an impasse. In *The Blind*, however, audiences are introduced to a dead father figure, that is, the breaking up of a heretofore harmonious approach to life. The images accompanying such a transformation, the "senex consciousness," are usually those of loneliness, isolation, rejection, and abandonment. It is interesting to note in this connection that Plato's dialogue with Socrates revolves around a dying man's attitude toward life and death and that Rembrandt, when in his twenties, painted a series of old people.[21]

In *The Blind* death is experienced as an encounter with the Father. He is the patriarchal force, a masculine principle that represents rational concepts and moral commandments. Maeterlinck's personal psychology at the time was experienced in terms of a negative father relationship. Unable to understand his son's inclinations, the father was forever repressing the young man's creative venture. He wanted him to practice law, and any deviation from the straight and narrow path was looked upon as a betrayal. Maeterlinck was burying the senex figure (the leader-priest) in his play while, symbolically speaking, permitting the creative impulse (the baby) within him to emerge.

A progression in terms of self-consciousness is implicit in *The Blind*. At the outset of the drama the protagonists await the priest's return. They listen for the slightest sound, and, though they feel disoriented ("We should know where we are"), they believe in their leader's imminent return. With the passage of time they begin to acknowledge their solitude. They comfort themselves with the illusion that rational knowledge will see them through the difficult period ahead: "We know very nearly everything one must know; let's chat a bit while waiting for the priest's return." Fear, nevertheless, intrudes: "I am afraid when I don't talk. . . ." Doubt in the future is now expressed. To allay their anguish, the blind have recourse to the past and believe that one day their present plight will also be a topic for discussion, ". . . one day I was looking at the snow from the top of a mountain . . ." declares one of the protagonists who was not born blind, "I was beginning to recognize those people who were unhappy . . . I have memories which are clearer when I do not think of them." Another protagonist, born blind, has no memories: "I, I have no souvenirs." at least no visible or tangible ones; only sensations, modulations, impressions. The protagonists then talk about a change in the priest's attitude during the years in the institution. After his friend's (the doctor's) death, he barely spoke at all. Perhaps "the rule of old men was going to end . . ." The patriarchal, or senex dynasty was drawing to a close.

As time grows heavy the group's mood alters. A growing impatience is discernible. They listen unnerved to the church clock striking midnight; noon? "Does anyone know? — Speak." They beseech those around them (the audience in this case) to answer their question and to share their anguish. Their need for audience participation is one of the earliest attempts on the part of a playwright to draw viewers into the play, a technique used with such felicity by Beckett, Genet, and Brecht. Since total silence follows the protagonists' agonizing plea, they decide to act on their own behalf. One of the blind men recalls that the priest had said they were near the river with its boats and sailors. They could perhaps attract someone's attention. "Does anyone want to follow me?" he asks. But no one ventures forth.

A gust of wind blows some leaves down from the dark mass of trees. The blind believe that something human has touched them. They listen more intently to the forest noises. They hear steps. A large dog comes on stage and passes in front of them. "Who is there? Who are you? — Have pity on us, have pity on us, we have been waiting for so long!" When the dog begins to lick one of them, the man realizes that it is a dog, but believes this animal has been sent to them by some outer worldly presence to deliver them from hunger. "He followed our tracks. He is licking my hands as if he had finally found me after so many centuries!"

Indeed, the dog has come to deliver the people, but not by taking them back to their institution. The dog is a harbinger of death. It has always been associated with death. According to the Aztec calendar, "the sign of the tenth day of Tonaltmatl" was a "dog. . . The regent of this sign was Miktlantekutli, the god of the dead." In ancient Egypt, Anubis, the Lord of the Grave, was represented as a dog, or jackal-headed god, who accompanied the dead to their domain. Shiva, the Hindu god of Creation and Destruction, was referred to as the "Lord of the Dogs."[22] A connection may also be made between the dog's devouring jaws and those of the earth. When the protagonists say, "I smell only the odor of the earth," they are in effect indicating an affinity with the earth in its capacity as devourer. In medieval French mystery plays the earth would frequently "open its jaws" and swallow up its victims, terrorizing many in the audience to the point of provoking heart attacks, miscarriages, births, and deaths.

The dog in Maeterlinck's drama leads one of the blind men to the dead priest. "There is a dead person in the midst of us!" the man declares. He discovers by a process of elimination the identity of the dead man. Now awareness of their existential plight takes hold of the twelve and with it, guilt begins to plague them. They had made their priest suffer; they had been too demanding; they had wanted to rest and eat during their journey whereas he had wanted to continue: "He lost courage."

The fact that the dead priest is resting against the "trunk of an enormous and cavernous oak tree" is also important. There are a variety of trees on stage: "large funereal" ones, yew trees, weeping willows, cypresses. The tree has always represented something sacred and awe-inspiring. The Celts, for example, considered the oak tree sacred; the Scandinavians, the ash. Gods were linked to all types of trees: Attis to the pine, Osiris to the cedar. Trees have stood for knowledge (Genesis), for the ten attributes of divinity (the Sefiroth in the Kabbala), and for sacrifice (Christ's cross). That the tree stands as a link between heaven and earth (its branches reaching up to the skies and its roots digging deep beneath the earth) may indicate man's rapport between his spiritual and instinctual sides. According to C. G. Jung, the tree is bisexual: the Latin endings of the names of trees are masculine despite the fact that their gender is feminine. The priest sitting at the base of the tree indicates his identification with it. He took on its attributes: totality, consistency, growth, proliferation, and the generative and regenerative process within nature. Because he is dead, his reign as a nutritive force, a spiritual guide, a protective power, or a divinity has ended.

After the discovery of the priest's death, the air chills. Terror grips the hearts of the blind. The stars vanish from the sky and snow begins to fall. The group huddles together, listening intensely for some sound, some indication of human life in the forest. Then the baby wails and the protagonists try to comfort it, to allay its fears. Footsteps are heard. Is it the leaves? the snow? Someone must be in their midst. They hold the baby over their heads so it can see for them. "Who are you?" a blind girl questions. Silence. "Have pity on us!" she cries out. An absence of sound envelops the atmosphere in sharp contrast to the desperate cry of the infant.

Maeterlinck's characters are transcendental. They live in a collective, mythical world. They bear no proper names and are divested of nearly all individuality save that some were blind at birth and others were not. As the six men sit opposite the six women, their elbows resting on their knees, their faces between their hands, they seem preoccupied with things beyond and above the routine of daily activities. "They have lost the habit of useless gesture and no longer turn their heads at the muffled and disquieting noises of the island." Eternal questions concern them now. The ephemeral world no longer exists.

The Blind is the story of a psychological crisis. It is a dramatic illustration of a dynamic progression that begins in a state of relative contentment and inertia, followed by a period of deep introversion and melancholia and continuing with fright at the confrontation with the dead father image. It concludes with the decay and disintegration of the "dying complex" — thus paving the way for a new orientation in terms of Maeterlinck's creative work as well as his personal life.

III The Seven Princesses — *The Creative Enigma*

So profound was Maeterlinck's depression in the spring of 1891 that he canceled his trip to Paris. Octave Mirbeau and Lugné-Poë were taken aback because they knew how much this city meant to him. Maeterlinck claimed to be suffering from heart palpitations; but when he finally consulted a physician in Brussels, he was given a clean bill of health and counseled to eat less and temper the richness of his food.

Depressed or not, Maeterlinck had settled down to a routine. He enjoyed the solitude of his small apartment in Brussels, which he had decorated with reproductions of pre-Raphaelite artists Edward Burne-Jones and Pierre Puvis de Chavannes, whose ethereal, pastel-toned canvases appealed to him. He spent much time writing. He also read, fraternized with his close friends at local cafés, took long walks or rode his bicycle. When the weather was nice, he went to Oostacker or visited his parents in Ghent.

Although Maeterlinck was becoming well known in a limited circle, he did not want to devote his life to writing, but thought of it as a happy outlet. He also vetoed the idea of pursuing his legal career. He did consider applying for some government post. His plans were quickly altered. His father's friends, well-placed in the government would have found him this sinecure, but they looked down on the writing profession. Their disdain and aloofness served Maeterlinck in good stead. The choice was no longer open, writing would be his career.

Maeterlinck's next play, *Les Sept Princesses* ("The Seven Princesses", 1891) was, he felt, not equal to his former works. Years later, at the height of his career, he did not consider it worthy of inclusion in his collected theatrical works.

The Seven Princesses, nevertheless, is a suspenseful and tightly knit drama. Each word, gesture, and insight has conciseness and depth and fits into the next, step by step. Its language is imagistic and flows freely in rhythmic cadences. The writing reveals in subdued archetypal images the real problems that beset the author at this juncture in his life, those of the creative artist wrestling to bring forth the new, searching for the inner core that mystics label the *point of creation*, where from nothing something emerges. Maeterlinck's play is a symbolic representation of the impasse he had reached in his writing career and of a blockage the dramatist sought to hide from audiences and critics alike, and perhaps even from himself.

The plot of *The Seven Princesses* is sparse. A king and queen of a northern country are in charge of seven beautiful princesses who have arrived from a distant, sun-drenched land. The royal couple is in despair because their wards have fallen asleep. Prince Marcellus has just returned from a seven-year sea venture and seeks to awaken the princesses. Encouraged by the royal pair, he tries to enter a glass-covered vault in the castle where they lie. The obstacle blocking his way to the princesses is too great to overcome at first; but after listening to the old king's advice, Marcellus finally reaches the princesses via another access. He awakens them all except for Ursule, the one in the center, the one he sought most. She is dead.

Kings and queens usually represent governing principles in fairy tales and myths. The pattern varies, however, in Maeterlinck's play. The royal couple in *The Seven Princesses*, as in *Princess Maleine*, is not endowed with the authoritative wisdom usually attributed to leaders. The king and queen are old, passive, sterile entities. Unable to prevent the princesses from going to sleep and fearful of awakening them, they keep a steady and anxious watch over them. The old couple are observers, not participants, in the drama and can do nothing to relieve or alter the condition of stasis. An external force, therefore, must intrude on this somnolent state of affairs to set things right, bringing new blood and fresh ideations and thereby renewing what has grown barren.

We are told that the princesses were always cold; that an oil lamp burned habitually near their beds so they would not be frightened by the darkness; that ever since their arrival they had been searching for the sun and light. According to Pythagorean mystics, cold and darkness are synonymous with death. The implication is that if the princesses were to continue to dwell in such an atmosphere, they would wither away. Southern climes have traditionally been associated with consciousness and the rational function, whereas northern regions have been likened to the unconscious and the unknown mystical realm. Because the princesses are enclosed as they sleep, they may be considered prisoners of a misty and dismal world over which reign a staid king and queen.

Psychologically speaking, the seven princesses represent Marcellus' *anima*, that is, his unconscious attitude to the personal and collective female figure, or, in religious terminology, to the soul image. Anima images have always appeared in literature and range from harlot to saint.[23] They are usually compensatory beings and represent what is lacking in the conscious orientation. In Marcellus's case, the princesses would represent feeling and the relating principle, Eros. As long as the seven princesses sleep (or remain unconscious), they will be envisaged as one vision, a fused entity in their "primal condition of perfection," and therefore unrecognizable to the conscious mind.[24]

We are told that after returning from a walk the princesses developed a high fever and fell into a deep sleep. Sleep was considered a healing process in many ancient lands. It was felt that repose permitted the poisons (or whatever was impeding the harmonious functioning of psyche and body) to depart, thereby leaving the individual free from disease. In ancient Greece, where there were more than three hundred dream-provoking or incubation centers under the aegis of the god Aesculapius, patients would follow a simple procedure: they would write down their ailments on a votive tablet, fall asleep in the sacred area within the temple, and

awake and relate their dream to the priest in charge, who would
then interpret it. If the sick person dreamed he had been visited by
a god, a cure was believed to be forthcoming; if not, he remained in
the temple until such time as a divinity appeared to him. In the
classical fairy tale *Sleeping Beauty*, the princess remains in a sleeping state until the arrival of the hero who then rouses her, and in so
doing cures her of her illness. By awakening her he also fulfills his
own potential by becoming aware of the unconscious contents he
has projected onto her. A working rapport between the unconscious
and the conscious comes into play, symbolically speaking; assimila-
tion of the new forces follows, enlarging the hero's existential frame
of reference.

In *The Seven Princesses* the pattern varies slightly. There are
seven anima figures (although these are lumped together) instead of
a single one, indicating a diffusion within the hero's primordial vision. The princesses are not enclosed in a remote tower but in a subterranean glass-covered vault; they remain visible at all times. A
container with water has been placed next to them should they be
thirsty upon awakening.

The number seven is of particular significance. Pythagoreans and
Platonist metaphysicians (Maeterlinck still pursued his studies of
the occult) believed that all within the cosmos could be reduced to
certain numerical figures. Numbers were considered the "essence of
harmony," the common denominator between man and the cosmos.
Seven is a composite of four (a whole number representing the soul
and without conflict, a number at rest) and three (a ternary number
representing the Christian and Buddhist godhead and perpetually
striving for completion, an active number). Seven therefore
becomes a *complexio oppositorum:* it includes activity and passivity, the finite and the infinite, the triangle placed over the square as
in the seven-pointed star. In that seven princesses are anima figures,
opposites live inchoate within them: movement and repose, strength
and weakness, health and sickness. Their constructive or destructive
aspects will emerge at one time or another, depending upon what
inner contents Marcellus projects upon them and the depth of his
projection.

The core of the drama revolves around Marcellus's attitude
toward the seven sleeping princesses. As he peers at them through
the misty glass window, he is at first mesmerized by their beauty

and delicacy. Although he can hardly tell one from the other, he slowly begins to distinguish one above the rest: Ursule, the tallest, who occupies the central position. Her features are blurred yet she is the one he seeks.

Ursule is the focal point of Marcellus' search. In religious rituals the central area (mandala, cross) remains the point of contemplation where inner and outer worlds meet, the spot where the transcendental (a state of mind) takes root in the phenomenological domain. The Greeks called the center of the earth *omphalos* ("navel"), that spot where unification between god, man, and death occurred. For the Buddhist, the center is that area in which construction and destruction, aspiration and expiration take place simultaneously.[25] For the Kabbalist and the mystic in general the center is considered the point of creation, the primordial point where nothing becomes something. Such an ideation has been explained in terms of the Hebrew word *ain* meaning "nothing", but which by rearranging the letters becomes *ani* or "I". The "I" is looked upon as the moment or point when God's personality "reveals itself to its own creation": the transformation from absence to substance, from the unmanifested to the manifested.[26] It is in this area that the unified becomes diffused, that cyclical is transformed into linear time, that spacelessness grows into spatial concepts. Just as the center is for the mystic the point of creation, so it is for the artist. It is at this juncture that the amorphous, nonlocalized, uncreated entity that precedes the creative act is converted into a concrete work of art. Marcellus has set himself the almost impossible task of rescuing the princesses, and in particular the one in the center. For the artist, this means to experience the creative content by rousing what is dormant and to exteriorize and concretize it in the work of art.

The glass vault in which the princesses are asleep is also significant. Just as the soul is held within the body and thought is encapsulated inside the brain, so the princesses are imprisoned (or protected) from the outside world. Glass, according to the Platonists, is like the eye: a mirror that permits access to the soul and thought, a bridge between the outer and inner worlds. The princesses, therefore, are visible at all times despite the fact that they are inactive. It is through glass, a transparent entity, that brightness enters the interior world and that light is shed onto the darkened realm where these anima figures sleep. In psychological terms, once what was unconscious or somnolescent is illuminated it is considered to have been brought into consciousness. The unconscious in this respect may be likened to a dark room cluttered with furniture. Once the electricity is turned on, the arrangement of the objects becomes clear, and one can walk about with ease. Glass and water images have frequently been linked to the Narcissus myth, and such an association is perfectly valid in terms of Maeterlinck's play. Narcissus fell in love with his own image reflected in a pool of water, plunged into the water to be united with it, and drowned in the process. Instead of looking at himself objectively, distinguishing between subject and object, thus erecting a bridge between the two and creating an energetic situation, Narcissus halted activity by fusing the two forces. In so doing he impeded any possible psychological development on his part; for this reason, heroes associated with the Narcissus myth are in most cases young men who have never gone beyond the adolescent stage. As Marcellus observes the maidens through the glass, he is in effect watching still dormant manifestations within his own unconscious. The question now arises as to his future relations with these entities. Will he remain enthralled by them or will he awaken them, relieving the inertia in the atmosphere, thus causing activity, and, hopefully creativity?

If Marcellus succeeds in freeing Ursule, he will really possess all seven princesses. The central point, the point of creation, is in effect the *fons et origo* of all future activity; it is subject neither to space nor time and therefore "contains all possibilities."[27] Just as all mankind is the prototype of the primordial or universal man, so the other sisters are merely manifestations of the one. Because Ursule is the focal point, the as yet unmanifested creative potential within the artist, she remains an abstraction, a thought, a mental state, a nonmaterial cosmic force, a transcendental and unique entity. Her image as such is blurred, vague, and ambiguous.

While trying to rescue the princesses the hero is confronted with a variety of obstacles, as is true in many fairy tales. Marcellus hears, for example, the song of the sailors in the distance as they chant their happiness while making ready to depart on their long voyage over the Atlantic. The rhythmic shouts of joy that inundate the stage are reminiscent of the melodies in Wagner's *The Flying*

Dutchman as the seafaring men make ready to leave for the high seas. But unlike the Flying Dutchman, Marcellus is not in search of sacrifice; rather he seeks to awaken the princesses, thus bringing to himself whatever they represent through projection into consciousness. He has already spent seven long years around the globe with the sailors and now has reached a new stage in his development and has a fresh orientation with regard to his creative output.

If Marcellus follows the sailors he will be "outward bound." He will continue to lead an extroverted existence, perhaps losing himself in the aggressive quest for worldly things. The sailors, as in Rimbaud's "Drunken Ship," travel about with no specific orientation and no purpose except their desire to break their ties with society and to see everything that lies beyond man's search. Because of such yearning they may be caught up in the vise of escapism and eventually devoured by their own *élan*. Interestingly enough, Maeterlinck's sailors are male counterparts of the ancient sirens. But unlike the sweet-singing creatures who enthralled and then destroyed the mariners who came within their reach, Maeterlinck's seafaring men lure their victims to a life of adventure — what they consider perpetual excitement — thereby rejecting responsibility, conflict, and maturity. Marcellus is caught between the outer world with its excitement and novelty and the inner realm with its haunting and alluring captives.

As soon as he decides on the introverted way, he enters the glass-enclosed area and descends the stairs leading to an ancient door. He fails in his attempt to open it because the door is locked from the inside. When the Queen sees Marcellus in such distress and hesitating in his purpose, she fears he might lose courage and give up. "Don't abandon them thus! . . . They have been sleeping for so long!" she implores.

Maeterlinck's prince in no way resembles the courageous heroes of the Siegfried type. The Norse fighter would have taken a hatchet to the door and destroyed it in one fell swoop. Maeterlinck's prince is more reasonable, more "civilized"; he is not guided exclusively by emotions and instincts; he does not act rashly and rather listens to the wisdom of the royal couple. The king points to another passage leading down to the princesses. He warns the entrance is narrow, stones must be lifted, and the darkness is all-encompassing. "But you must know the way . . . . You have gone down there more than once in the past." The implication is that Marcellus has already accomplished the journey to the realm beneath in the past.

Whenever an impasse is reached in one's temporal attitude a retreat into the inner world is salutary. With introversion the psychic energy usually expended in coping with daily pursuits flows inward rather than outward, activating certain somnolent contents within the unconscious. When such a reshuffling takes place, inner activity causes new images and fresh forces to come into consciousness, thereby enlarging and altering existential views.

As Marcellus's attitude changes, so does the royal couple's. The King, formerly innocuous, now assumes a more active role in the drama. He becomes a kind of spiritual guide, a psychopomp, a mana personality representative of wisdom and reflection. Marcellus follows the King's advice, acts "rationally", and enters the inner domain slowly with circumspection. Having accepted wisdom as his "mentor", his gestures are measured; his way is that of the higher or spiritual personality;[28] his so-called "primitive" world of instinct has been devalued. It is just this breach within Marcellus's psyche and temporal attitude that will prevent him from fulfilling his potential and reviving Ursule.

Like a "hunter of souls," Marcellus, so reminiscent of Orpheus in this respect, acts under the guidance of parental figures and rescues the princesses from a kind of underworld. The King and Queen observe from above through the glass window as an inner world slowly becomes inundated with light. Only six princesses awaken; Ursule, the center figure, remains lifeless. The seven years she waited for her prince were too long, and she had grown tired and sick from lack of attention — that is, the creative element within the artist had literally died of neglect. Creativity requires activity and conflict.

When seven becomes six (or an odd becomes an even number), Marcellus is divested of opposition. Excitement and imbalance, which had compelled him to forge on in his quest, are replaced by equilibrium and calm. An impasse had now been reached.

An analogy may be drawn between Maeterlinck's dramatic productions during the year 1890: *Princess Maleine*, *The Intruder*, and *The Blind* were all despairing plays dealing almost exclusively with death. With *The Seven Princesses*, however, Maeterlinck succeeded in rousing the point of creativity symbolized by Ursule.

The Seven Princesses, then, illuminated Maeterlinck's inner world and shed light on what previously was obscured by darkness — that which had been barren. Ursule, the anima figure, stirred the dramatist, paving the way for the masterpiece that followed, *Pelléas and Mélisande*.

IV Pelléas and Mélisande — *The Spirit of Eros and Anteros*

Pelléas et Mélisande, directed by Lugné-Poë, was first produced on May 17, 1893, at the Bouffes-Parisiens.

Aurélien Lugné, a devotee of Symbolism at the outset of his career, had added the name of Poë to his own, claiming he was a distant relative of the American poet. In reality, however, it was out of respect and admiration for the writer who had introduced him to a world of mystery and the occult and who had been Baudelaire's "mystic brother." Refused entry to the Conservatoire, Lugné-Poë would not be stopped from an acting career and joined Paul Fort's Théâtre d'Art. At the same time, he began cultivating a group of painters known as the Nabis.

The name Nabis was taken from the Hebrew word meaning "prophet." The Nabis group included such painters as Pierre Bonnard, Edouard Vuillard, Ker-Xavier Roussel, Félix Valloton, Paul Sérusier and Maurice Denis, all destined to become well known. These young artists had left the Académie Julian in 1890, rejecting the conventional concepts, the formalized ways, and the stereotyped vision advocated by this school. Lugné-Poë, who was not only an excellent actor but also a fine writer, helped the Nabis by writing articles about their canvases. This helped to sell them, or at least made the artists known to friends and acquaintances in the acting and literary world.

It was not character that was important to the Nabis, nor infinite detail, but as Denis, the spokesman of the group, said after looking at one of Gauguin's canvases: "Thus we learn that all art is a transposition, the impassioned counterpart of an experienced sensation." And he continued: "Remember that a picture before being a battle horse, a nude, an anecdote, or whatnot, is essentially a flat surface covered with colors assembled in a certain order. "The Nabis painted on cardboard and blended turpentine with their pigment, thereby lending a "mat" effect to the surface. They applied cool colors and warm tones, rather than brilliant and harsh hues.

Vuillard advocated indecisiveness, vagueness, and quoted Verlaine's famous dictum: "Où l'indécis au précis se joint." A simplification of character was recommended, a sober attitude, an abandonment of harsh realism and explicitly delineated objects and people. Muted tones, neutral colors, a vagueness of atmosphere was their goal.[29]

Lugné-Poë in many ways applied the Nabis's conception of painting to his theatrical productions. His innovative procedures with regard to *Pelléas and Mélisande*, for example, caused quite a stir. Flat and muted tones were *de rigueur*. The stage was for the most part bathed in darkness, contrary to the custom. Only diffused and dim rays shone here and there on the proscenium. The footlights were also done away with, to create a closer rapport between audience and actors. All extraneous accessories and sets were banished. A gauze veil was placed across the stage, emphasizing the play's spiritual quality, dreaminess, and mystery.[30]

The vagueness, ambiguity, and outer-worldly impression achieved by such a technique aroused the admiration of one of France's leading writers, Octave Mirbeau, Maeterlinck's earliest champion. The coloring onstage, he wrote, was "graduated in muted tones of dark blue, mauve, and blue-greens of the actors costumes." The dim nuances, so reminiscent of the canvases of Puvis de Chavannes, were evocative, suggestive, and not explicative. Theodor de Wyzewa's description of the French pre-Raphaelite artist's paintings could also be applied to Maeterlinck's drama: "We are struck by a thirst for dreams, for emotions, for poetry. Satiated with light, too vivid and too crude, we longed for fog. And it was then that we attached ourselves passionately to the poetic and misty art of Puvis de Chavannes."[31]

The chiaroscuro on the proscenium, in direct opposition to the realism and naturalism of the time, stimulated the dream world and was instrumental in paving the way for a whole new orientation in the theater. The strange happenings, which took place in a forest, in subterranean passageways, became visual expressions of pictorial patterns existing in the unconscious, giving form in this manner to archetypal images and embodying these visualisations in a series of rhythmic and poetic progressions.

Pelléas and Mélisande is a fairy tale. Its central theme is the birth and burgeoning of love and the destruction of the protagonists by passion. Love, or Eros, understood philosophically not only represents the attraction one person feels for another, but also symbolizes a unifying force in nature. Anteros, on the other hand, Eros's brother, the god of unrequited love (always overcome with bitterness and anguish), seeks revenge and is known as the agent of discord, the dismemberer of all that is linked in the cosmos. According to Pythagorean metaphysics, which Maeterlinck had studied, the world (or any creative act) was born out of discord or chaos (Anteros), evolved under the dictates of Eros, ossified, and became sterile, thus paving the way for the spirit of Anteros to again take hold, to separate what had been unified, to make rebirth and renewal possible. According to such concepts, there are periods in history as well as in human relationships when Eros (relatedness) prevails and other times when Anteros (discontinuity) reigns.

Eros and Anteros are the forces and counterforces that make for the peripeteia and lysis of the fairy tale *Pelléas and Mélisande*. Unlike the myth, which focuses on cultural patterns, the fairy tale is divested of all extraneous material.[32]

The plot of *Pelléas and Mélisande* is simple. Golaud, the grandson of Arkel, lord of a manor, is out hunting. He sees a young girl in the forest, Mélisande, who comes from a distant land. En route she has lost her crown, which Golaud offers to search for, but she no longer wants it. Golaud and Mélisande marry and go to his somber castle by the sea. Here Mélisande meets Golaud's young brother, Pelléas, who was supposed to leave on a journey to visit a dying friend. His mother Geneviève has requested he remain at the castle because of his father's serious illness. Arkel accepts Mélisande into the family although he had hoped for a politically more advantageous union to bring riches to the famine-stricken community. Yniold, Golaud's little son by his first marriage, is always at Mélisande's side. Pelléas and Mélisande fall in love. One afternoon Mélisande loses her wedding ring while playing with it at the edge of a fountain. Golaud observes the entente between Pelléas and Mélisande and grows jealous. He has Yniold spy on the lovers, surprises them in each other's arms, kills Pelléas, and wounds Mélisande. She dies shortly after giving birth to a pitifully tiny baby girl.

The tragic love motif in *Pelléas and Mélisande* has been compared to the devastating passion experienced by Paolo and Francesca da Rimini, to Othello's blind love for Desdemona, and to

Poe's child lovers in "Annabel Lee."

> I was a child and she was a child,
>   In this kingdom by the sea,
> But we loved with a love that was more than love —
> I and my Annabel Lee.

Pelléas and Mélisande has also been likened to the Tristan and Isolde legend. Yet there is a difference between the two. In *Pelléas and Mélisande* love is experienced unconsciously; the rational principle is all but abolished; the existential situation is not taken into consideration and destruction quite naturally ensues. Moreover, unlike in medieval legends, there are no magic brews in *Pelléas and Mélisande*, no natural forces (like calm or stormy seas) to intrude on the drama. But fate or what Maeterlinck looked upon as the Gnostic *heimarmene*, does make its presence felt. Some mysterious force compels the childlike protagonists to spin their web of destruction openly, relentlessly, and conclusively. Eros predominates to such a degree that blindness reigns and distance cannot be experienced; barriers vanish and codes of ethics are forgotten. Anteros's wrath is aroused, bringing with it death and an end to an unbalanced psychological attitude.

The fairy tale structure with its obstacles, inexplicable appearances and disappearances, and its unaccountable dangers seems the perfect vehicle to cause bonds to be created (Eros) and broken (Anteros) in order to dramatize Maeterlinck's metaphysical concepts.

As the play progresses, we learn that a famine rages throughout the region. People are dying; disease is rampant, agitation and a spirit of rebellion mark the atmosphere. When aridity and chaos prevail in fairy tales, it is usually an indication of the unproductive nature or sterile point of view in the ruling attitude. A need for change is expressed in the feelings of dissatisfaction with the status quo; renewal is imperative or further decay will come to pass. Anteros, therefore, must begin to break up the stratified, ingrown, and barren conditions in both the physical and spiritual domains.

The first clue to the evil fate to befall the protagonists occurs in the opening scene of *Pelléas and Mélisande*. The servants are washing the doorstep leading into the castle. Despite the fact that they bring a lot of water and scrub hard, they seem discouraged and claim they "will never be able to wash all of this clean," the impurities on the threshhold of Golaud's castle remain embedded in the stone.

The forest scene that follows is of extreme importance. Golaud has lost his way. Such a lack of orientation may indicate an inner need to transcend the confines of his existence and transform the worn pattern of his life. He comes upon a girl standing next to a fountain. She is petrified. "Don't touch me!" she says, or "I'll throw myself into the water!"[33] She is lost. More important, perhaps, is the fact that she has mislaid her crown and does not want the stranger to retrieve it. Mélisande's appearance in the forest is not explicable along rational lines. Her being lost reveals a confusion, and her unwillingness to look for her crown spells a desire to dissociate herself from her past. When Golaud asks detailed questions about Mélisande's family, her nation, and so on, her answers are vague and ambiguous as if she herself were not sure of them.

It is not by chance that Golaud finds Mélisande next to a fountain. Since medieval times, and even before, the fountain has always represented the infinite possibilities that await a person when starting out in life or on a creative venture. Mélisande is childlike, nonworldly; she has appeared almost magically on the scene as in any fairy tale domain. She is pure, naïve, and graceful, and wears the intangible, remote, and passive features of the women depicted by Burne-Jones. Two possibilities are given to Golaud in his encounter with Mélisande: either Eros or Anteros can take over his existence.

Mélisande may be looked upon as an anima figure (a soul image). She is therefore revelatory of Golaud's feelings and unconscious state. Her presence indicates, to a certain degree, the void in his life: its lack of beauty, radiance, tenderness, and idealism. Because Golaud projects his unconscious ideal on Mélisande, he is unable to differentiate between his vision of her and the real person. His relationship with her, therefore, can never evolve and will always remain on a superficial level. Mélisande comments at the outset of their meeting on his graying hair, an indication of the course of their relationship: father-daughter (creator-creation), never husband and wife (mutual understanding).

That both get lost in the forest is revelatory of their lack of vision.

Because a forest is usually dark and large, it has been associated with the unconscious; thickly wooded and fertile, it has also been linked to the Great Mother, the female principle in nature that causes growth. In many fairy tales monstrous forms appear in forests and a forbidding atmosphere is created. In *Pelléas and Mélisande* the opposite is true: Golaud has a vision and sees the exquisitely beautiful girl in the purity, luster, and freshness of youth. But being the personification of his ideal female figure, she will never take on any reality. She is not of this world and is in no way related to it.

Patriarchal forces predominate once Golaud and Mélisande arrive at the castle. All in the province are subservient to Arkel, Golaud's grandfather and the lord of the region. Golaud fears that Arkel may not be satisfied with the marriage to Mélisande. Arkel had wanted him to conclude an economically profitable union that would bring wealth to the sterile land. But when Arkel sees Mélisande, he is won over immediately: her purity, gentleness, and little-girl qualities enthrall him. Mélisande is the Eros principle par excellence. It is she who can bring all disparate factors together.

The brother motif is common in fairy tales and myths (Cain and Abel, Osiris and Set). Brothers usually represent dual aspects of the same figure. Pelléas and Golaud are brothers but of different fathers. Golaud, the hunter, is aggressive and extroverted. He goes out to "catch" his prey — his bride. Pelléas, on the other hand, is passive and introverted, and permits things to happen. He adheres to his mother's request not to leave home.

The first time Pelléas and Mélisande converse, the personalities of both protagonists begin to emerge. With Pelléas Mélisande is no longer submissive and fearful as she is with Golaud. On the contrary, she becomes a dominant factor. She acts in a provocative, seductive, playful way, and taunts Pelléas. Despite his warning, she plays with her wedding ring above the water. Indeed, she takes on certain attributes of the siren: alluring, mesmerizing, dangerous.

Siren myths and tales are found in medieval bestiaries as well as in the works of Aristotle, Pliny, and Ovid. The French have their own siren, Mélusine. (We note the similarity in sounds between Mélusine and Mélisande.) The siren has come to represent the inferior forces of woman, those forces that entice men to enter the most primitive levels of existence, leading inevitably to self-destruction. The siren incarnates the earth principle (instinct) rather than the rational aspect (spirit) and is therefore governed by the moon. Mélisande, throughout the drama, seeks the darkness of the night. Sirens are also associated with water, as is to be expected, and so is Mélisande: the fountain scene and the imagery throughout the drama likens her to water. Mélisande, then, will be the instigator, the *agente provocatrice*, in the play of events.

The fountain beside which Pelléas and Mélisande talk is ancient and abandoned. Pelléas alludes to it as "the miraculous fountain" and "the fountain of the blind" because it enables the sightless to see.[34] Interestingly, the fountain has also been associated with life as is stated in the thirty-sixth Psalm. "For with thee is the fountain of life: in thy light shall we see light." The fountain, representing the source of life, activity, and potentiality, also stands for the unconscious or the center of the spiritual world, the soul. It is a realm *in potentia* and is sought when people's existential situation has become arid. To immerse oneself in water is to regress to a preformal state and in this way to start anew, to be reborn. Such was Golaud's situation before Mélisande's arrival. She has become a source of renewal and rejuvenation for him. The relationship which came into existence has gone askew, however; it is unbalanced and is not spiritually fruitful. When Mélisande again comes to the fountain, to be rebaptized, she seeks to experience an initiation into another frame of existence.

In the fountain scene Mélisande complains that her "hands are sick"[35]; an indication that her "active," or worldly, outlook is not functioning properly. She plays with her ring, which drops into the water. Because the marriage band is circular, it is considered a symbol of eternity and wholeness and in this sense resembles the Gnostic image of the *ouroborus* or the snake biting its own tail. Circular forms indicate an infantile state, in psychological terms the ego is still identified with the self, that is, before differentiation and consciousness have come into being. Mélisande's desire to rid herself of the ring may be regarded as a rejection of her marriage and submissive relationship with Golaud.

Maeterlinck, who believed in extrasensory perception and in synchronistic events, gives us an example of how linear and spatial time concepts are transcended: while Golaud is hunting in the forest, he is thrown from his horse at the very instant Mélisande's ring drops into the water. "I thought my heart had been crushed," he tells her later in the castle when recovering from his wounds.[36] At this juncture Mélisande utters her Cassandra-like prognostications. She will die, she tells him, if she remains in the castle; she must leave. Golaud cannot respond in rational terms to her request since he does not understand its import. He responds in chiaroscuro imagery: "It is true this castle is very old and very sombre. . . . It is cold and deep. . . . And the countryside seems very sad, too, with all of its forests, all of those old forests without lights."[37]

When Golaud discovers the loss of Mélisande's ring, he is overcome with grief: "I would have preferred to have lost everything I own than to have lost that ring." The ring has become a hierophany for him: a sacred object, a manifestation of divinity, a concretization of the anima. To be divested of the ring means to sever his union with Mélisande or, in psychological terms, to destroy his projection (his ideal), to cleave what has been unified. His fall from the horse and his bloodied face are external expressions of his inner wound.[38]

Instead of telling Golaud the truth about her loss Mélisande claims she lost the ring in the underground vaults. He sends her there forthwith and asks Pelléas to accompany her. Mélisande fears the darkness of the subterranean passages, the perils awaiting the unwary every step of the way, and the narrow paths with the deep ravines on either side. "It is filled with tenebrous blues. Its depths have never been explored. Treasures, it seems, have been hidden there."[39] Blackness, underground recesses are frequently looked upon as symbols of the "heart" as well as the unconscious. In these somber and dangerous recesses treasures exist that may provide great wealth if properly assimilated by the conscious mind and channeled into one's existential existence. If improperly understood, however, they may bring about destruction to the uninitiated traveler.

After the grotto experience Pelléas and Mélisande express their love for one another. Yniold, Golaud's son by his first wife, inadvertently tells his inquisitive father of the trysts between the lovers. The balcony scene follows, so reminiscent of *Romeo and Juliet*. Mélisande leans over the railing and lets her hair fall on Pelléas below. He kisses her hair and talks to it as if it were alive: "It is lukewarm and tender as if it had fallen from heaven. . . . Look, look at it, my hands can hardly hold it. . . . It escapes me, it escapes and bends into the weeping willows."[40] Golaud sees his brother and his wife and is annoyed: "You are children. . . . Don't play this way in the dark."

Golaud and Pelléas walk together in the subterranean vaults beneath the castle. Abysses, pits, dangers are all about. Pelléas does not know his way around, Golaud does. Although Golaud seethes with jealousy, he does not throw his brother into a ravine. His anger has not yet overwhelmed him to the point of committing the criminal act; on the contrary, he takes hold of his brother's arm to prevent him from slipping into a pit. Pelléas, unlike his brother, is stifled by the atmosphere and finds breathing difficult. The underground vaults are intolerable. The discomfort Pelléas experiences is a physical manifestation of his psychological state: the growing awareness of the dangers involved if his relationship with Mélisande is to continue. Golaud, in fact, warns him outright to keep away from her. She is expecting a child, he says, "and the least emotion could bring about misfortune."[41]

Pelléas decides to leave the castle and to venture forth on his own. Had he taken into account the premonitory sensations he experienced in the subterranean vault scene (the feeling of claustrophobia), he would not have asked Mélisande to meet him one last time at the fountain. At this rendezvous the drama reaches its climax. By having confessed their passion for one another, the lovers retreat into the unconscious realm. They do not take into consideration the dangers involved in their *regressus ad uterum*. The imagery stresses such a withdrawal when Pelléas compares Mélisande's voice to water: "Your voice! your voice . . . is fresher and more frank than water. . . . "[42] He asks her to come into the light, away from the shadow of the trees.[43] She, however, prefers to remain in the tenebrous zones, another instance of her identification with the moon and the principles it represents: the unconscious and irrational associated with feminine psychology. Pelléas is forever seeking light; the sun principle, the judging, rational, and masculine point of view. Darkness prevails. Love (Eros) permits Pelléas and Mélisande to dwell in the undifferentiated world of childhood, to become reintegrated into a fabulous era, a mythological past. As they stand beside the "Miraculous Fountain" in their embrace, Golaud surprises them. He kills Pelléas and wounds Mélisande. Unlike Cain's murder of Abel, which was com-

mitted in all innocence (it was the first murder on earth and conse-
quences of violence were not yet known), Golaud understands his
destructive act.[44] He has severed what had been so well knit and has
paved the way for renewal, which occurs with the birth of
Mélisande's child. But who is the father? Golaud or Pelléas? The
question remains unanswered.

Pelléas and Mélisande is an example in dramatic form of the conflict between Eros, life's cyclical process and the cohesive forces it
brings into existence, and Anteros, a power capable of severing bonds
in order to recreate new ones, thus enabling universal rhythms to
pursue their course. As Antonin Artaud stated, "Maeterlinck's
philosophy is like a temple in action" — it is of cosmic dimension.

Maeterlinck was so nervous on opening night, he did not attend
the performance. Instead, he walked about the Palais Royal area.
The critics, the old guard, were unanimous in their disapproval.
Jules Lemaître found the interest flagging. Francisque Sarcey, one
of the most important critics of the period, wrote in *Le Temps* (May
22, 1893):

Ah! yes, that's the mistake in the play; everyone is mysterious, everything
takes on an air of mystery. One emerges from such a tenebrous area an absolute dolt, as though one were wearing a lead skull cap on one's head.

The Symbolists — Mallarmé, Mirbeau, and others — saw in
Pelléas and Mélisande the theater of the future. The poet Henri de
Régnier, a friend of Maeterlinck, spoke of the play to the then unknown and impoverished composer Claude Debussy. Maeterlinck
gave Debussy permission to compose an operatic score to it. In
August 1893 Debussy set to work on what would become his
greatest opera — and it would add to Maeterlinck's fame the world
over.

CHAPTER 3

A Theater for Marionettes

F OR a number of years Maeterlinck had been drawn to the world of the marionette, as had been some notable predecessors — namely, Chaucer, Shakespeare, and Goethe. Marionettes and puppets are very ancient. They were used in Greece in the fifth century B.C. In Europe throughout the Middle Ages they became the most popular form of entertainment for the masses. But the Orientals brought this art to its apogee. In the formalized Japanese Bunraku (puppet theater), each figure is worked by three men dressed in black and wearing masks; in the East Javanese and Balinese Wayang Kulit (shadow theater), the manipulator of the one-dimensional dolls used to be regarded as a spiritual guide, the representative of outer-worldly forces, a symbol of destiny.

At this juncture of his career, Maeterlinck felt that human actors, because they were restricted by their physical characteristics, were not appropriate vehicles to portray the archetypal figures with which he peopled his stage. Since wooden dolls were complex and ambiguous forces, they infused a super- or extrahuman dimension into the stage happenings. Inhabitants of two worlds, the real and the unreal, they could be transformed into anything at any time: god or man, saint or sinner. Like phantoms, they strutted about and stirred, terrified, and pained in a strangely inhuman way those who viewed them. Marionettes came to life only when the spectator projected his unconscious content onto them.

What impressed Maeterlinck in particular was the passive, remote, impersonal and automatonlike nature of the marionette as it fruitlessly confronted the forces of destiny. He saw an analogy between man and the marionette: both are manipulated by outer forces, both are unaware of this control over their lives. The marionette is directed by the puppeteer; man is the plaything of the gods. Thee stage is a microcosm of the macrocosm.

Rather than accepting his subservience to outer-wordly forces, man deceives himself into believing he is a *homo faber*. He identifies with the manipulator of the dolls and is infused with feelings of inflation. For Maeterlinck, marionettes were perfect vehicles to demonstrate man's weakness when confronted with the forces of heimarmene. It confirmed Schopenhauer's ideations as formulated in *The World* as *Will and Idea* (1818), a book Maeterlinck had read again and again. Schopenhauer claimed that man's will, over which he has virtually no control, is the source of his unhappiness. It is *will* that forces him to strive and to wish for the impossible. Dissatisfaction, frustration, and anguish always ensue. Only by suppressing or controlling the will through the intellect, that is, by diminishing or overcoming desire and want, can terrestrial needs be transcended, thus making possible the achieving of a peaceful and painless state of pure contemplation. The artist, by molding his work of art, must not create forms embedded in the ephemeral domain, which alter with each political, social, or artistic regime; rather, he must go beyond these entities and formulate something that exists outside the world of necessity.

It was these points, the marionettes' archetypal or collective nature, their ambiguity and mystery, their helplessness and their power, that motivated Maeterlinck to write three plays for marionettes: *Alladine et Palomides* ("Alladine and Palomides"), *Intérieur* ("Interior"), and *La Mort de Tintagiles* ("The Death of Tintagiles," 1894).

I   Alladine and Palomides

Alladine and Palomides has been looked upon as an extension of *Pelléas and Mélisande* and nothing more. Even Maeterlinck stated that his play was a "decoction of *Pelléas*." Each is a *pittura metafisica*. Both dramas are enacted in a remote decor, removed from the workaday world; they take place in some dim past, some mythological domain. The characters, exiled from nineteenth-century industrial society, resemble subliminal forces, shadows hovering over a beclouded scene.

The old King Ablamore is to marry the young and beautiful Alladine. His daughter, Astolaine, a spiritual and self-abnegating figure, is affianced to Palomides. Astolaine's wedding is to take place in three days. Palomides arrives at the king's castle, meets Alladine, and they fall in love. He tells Astolaine of his change of heart. She understands this, accepts it, and withdraws from the marriage vows. Her father, however, is angered. He feels his daughter's pain vicariously, he declares, and his pride is hurt, too; because Alladine loves another. He has Alladine and Palomides walled into the grotto under his castle, then he vanishes. Alladine and Palomides fall into the water-filled abyss in the underground vaults and are rescued by Astolaine and Palomides's sisters. But it is too late; the couple dies from an "incurable disease."

Ablamore is pictured as a wise king who has ruled his country and his people with love and kindness. From the outset, however, the audience senses that some misfortune is about to befall this monarch. When, for example he looks at his future bride, the sleeping Alladine, he murmurs: "It is sad to love too late."[1] Alladine's eyes are beautiful, he says, but only when they look at others. When turned his way, they take on a hard, glazed look.[2] According to Platonic belief, eyes are mirrors of the soul. Thus they reveal Alladine's true — but yet unconscious — feelings. They cannot deceive. Plotinus considered eyes as the human counterpart of the sun, a radiating force, a light-bringing factor within man. It is via her eyes that Alladine's inner world is exteriorized and her ideations are exposed. Her eyes indicate that something is amiss. The age discrepancy between the young Alladine and the old king is one factor, destiny is another.

When Alladine awakens, she does so with a start, as if roused from an unfortunate dream. She is fearful of her situation and surroundings; terrified, for one thing, of the infinite number of rooms in the palace, and the palace's twisting and turning corridors in which she has gotten lost countless times. Once she had opened thirty doors before seeing the light of the day, and even then the last door opened onto a pond that prevented her from stepping out of the palace. Everything about Ablamore's palace represents darkness, decay, constriction. Spiritually and physically, she is bound and fettered. In such a negative patriarchal atmosphere the young Alladine cannot evolve. She is crushed, overwhelmed, lost, so to speak, in the maze of Ablamore's ways. Totally disoriented, Alladine cannot find her way out of her predicaments. Danger is present no matter which castle door she opens.

Alladine and Palomide are made of the same metal. They are earth creatures. Each is associated, for example, with an animal. Alladine has her pet lamb, Palomides his horse. The lamb is usually considered a symbol of sacrifice. It was first encountered in Hebrew apocalyptic literature (*The Book of Enoch*), later it was incorporated into Christian symbolism as the Lamb of God or Christ. The lamb is meek, unaggressive, and docile, as is Alladine. She yields to everyone: first to Ablamore or what he represents, the spiritual father image, then to Palomides, the world of instinct. The lamb is also associated with alchemical symbology: the lamb or *agnus*, is connected with *agni*, meaning "fire." As a fire symbol, Alladine may be thought of as a catalyzing agent. Her lamb or agni represents a volatile, active force that paves the way for a change of attitude, a transformation of situations, a transmutation of relationships as in the alchemical process. When in one scene, Palomides' horse, after returning from a hunting trip, pushes Alladine's lamb aside, one may conclude that the world of instinct and the world of fire (both similar) are destined to meet and perhaps destroy one another. The horse, an agent of instinct is also associated with Mars, the war god. Palomides, passionate and chaotic, is in effect, declaring war against Alladine, as attested to in the drawbridge scene. Palomides has called the lamb, which in its haste falls off the drawbridge.[3] Rather than attempting to rescue the lamb, Palomides, much to Alladine's distress, lets it drown in the moat. The fire has died. The war is, symbolically, over. It is only a matter of time before destiny carries out its inexorable dictates.

Ablamore sees his daughter as the essence of kindness. When she learns of Palomides's change of heart, she accepts it with grace, and even encourages Palomides in his relationship with Alladine. The king, however, is not so magnanimous. He seeks revenge and uses the excuse that he has to protect his daughter "who fears to trouble with a tear, or even with the movement of an eyelash, the happiness of those surrounding her."[4]

Palomides does not love Astolaine in a mortal way; rather, he worships her. She is an anima figure, a projection of his ideal inner image of a woman. When he approaches her, it is as though he were "opening a window onto dawn. . . . She has a soul that radiates, that takes you in its arms like a suffering child . . . consoles you in all ways."[5] There is no common denominator between Astolaine and Palomides. She is spirit, he is earth. She hovers about his world as does a phantasmagoria, an idealization, a truly sacrificial figure who attempts to bring peace to all around.

Astolaine is a modern incarnation of all the positive aspects of Isis, Aphrodite, and the Virgin Mary in one. She encompasses "all that could be considered tender kindness and the perfect simplicity of a woman."[6] Until he met her, Palomides had lived a peripheral existence as if "enclosed in a room." Now, he confesses, he "weeps with admiration" at her gestures, her smile: "You are the soul of everyone." Those who have not known Astolaine have not experienced the extreme beauty of life. Through her Palomides has learned to expand his vision, to see life beyond its physical limitations.

However, once Palomides has viewed both sides of existence, he breaks with her. She is too perfect an individual, too remote, too celestial. No real relationship can be enjoyed between the two. He is unworthy of her, as man is unworthy of an angel. "Have pity on me," he says. He knows Alladine to be inferior to Astolaine; she is endowed with "a child's soul, the soul of a poor weak child" and by comparison with the sublime Astolaine she is nothing. Yet he cannot resist the inferior woman.[7] Palomides cries; not Astolaine. He experiences the guilt and the conflict that come once both facets of life emerge into consciousness.

The love Astolaine inspires is superhuman. In many respects she is comparable to Violaine and Palomides to Jacques in Claudel's *The Announcement made to Mary*. Astolaine is capable only of a metaphysical, a Platonic relationship, not a mortal bond. To prefer such a love is to live a saintly existence and to reject human nature, turning away from instinct and sensuality that are inherent in *homo sapiens*. Palomides cannot nor will not reject this side of himself. He longs for the child in man, the carefree, happy existence he believes he would know with Alladine.

Astolaine is cognizant of her nature. She tells her father of her change of heart and says she cannot love as ordinary people do. Like Balzac's *ange-femme* or his hermaphroditic Seraphita-Seraphitus, she transcends the world of matter. She longs to see Alladine and Palomides happy together.

Ablamore, nevertheless, locks up the couple in his subterranean grotto — similar to the fate of Antigone and Haman. Strength and

ingenuity enable Palomides to free them both of the cloths that
cover their eyes and the cords that bind their hands. They are daz-
zled by the light shining within the grotto. "You seem to be on the
edge of a limitless clarity."[8] They believe they have seen *reality* for
the first time, they have peered through the veneer of the
phenomenological world. The light within the grotto grows steadily
brighter; a firelike illumination greets them as if this underworld
domain had been ignited by a flame.[9] Such a light (like the lamb
symbol earlier in the play) represents the heat of passion, the
alchemical fire used to transmute metals, the Heraclitean warmth
that is the basis of creation itself. Alladine and Palomides experience the full scope of their instinctual chaotic realm in their
grotto world. They view the unfolding world of beauty with
tremulous joy. They "needed this eternal light" in order to bring
this tremendous passion to consciousness. "I want to see the kisses
tremble in your heart."[10] As they become aware that they are standing over a high cliff above the water, they realize the dangers involved in such an all-consuming passion. Rocks suddenly begin to
fall. The grotto is invaded by another light: unbearable and harsh,
revealing the poverty and ugliness of the subterranean area they
had first thought so beautiful. The light overwhelms them. They
fall into the abyss below and are rescued by Astolaine and
Palomides's sisters, who had burrowed through the wall. After the
couple is brought to their rooms, the doctor declares them incurable. The terrestrial passion they suffered is a fatal sickness as in
the case of Tristan who also died for love. The audience now hears
the voices of Alladine and Palomides calling weakly to each other
from their rooms — as if reaching out from two distinct worlds:
"One would think that yours [voice] has traversed death. . . ."

   Alladine and Palomides dramatizes the conflict between a "fiery"
earthly passion (which is so all-consuming that it blocks out all other
forces in life) and an overly spiritual attitude. Interestingly,
Maeterlinck introduces audiences to a new personality type: the actively self-sacrificing individual who unwittingly, because of an un-
worldly attitude, helps bring on the calamitous end. Heretofore
Maeterlinck's protagonists were childlike or passive individuals sub-
mitting to their fate rather than trying to order it according to their
views.

II Interior

Interior, performed successfully at the Théâtre de l'Oeuvre on March 15, 1895, is a meditation on death. Maeterlinck may have been moved to write this play after the death in 1891 of his young brother Oscar from double pneumonia contracted after a skating accident.[11]

The action of the play takes place in a house, visible from the three ground-floor windows, and in a garden in front of the mansion. The family inside the house consists of a father, a mother holding a baby in her lap, and two young girls dressed in white. These characters do not speak, they merely rise, walk, and gesticulate in "grave, slow, sparse" ways as though they had been "spiritualized by distance."[12] In the garden are an Old Man, his two daughters, and a Stranger. They talk, trying to determine the best way of breaking the terrible news to the seemingly peaceful family within: the death by drowning of a daughter.

A new feature in this play is the great emphasis placed on mimetic art. The dialogue in the garden is almost exclusively a series of comments and conversations concerning the family in the house. A close rapport, therefore, exists between the emotions expressed by the Old Man and the Stranger and the bodily movements of the people within. The dissociation of speech and action, novel for the period, breaks to a certain extent the conventional empathy usually existing between actor and audience. Although distance separates the two groups, the emotions and thoughts articulated by the Old Man and the Stranger are in an unusual way sometimes sensed by those in the house and mirrored by their pantomime, in a kind of "active silence."[13] When, for example, the Old Man and the Stranger speak of the corpse that was found in the lake, the two sisters in the house turn their heads toward the window as though echoing some mysterious feeling, some excruciating presentiment.

A sense of secrecy and uneasiness pervades the atmosphere. The young girl's death is mysterious. Had she wanted to die? The Stranger says the peasants had seen her wandering by the river. They thought she was looking for a certain flower. Or was she? The Old Man insinuates the possibility of suicide: "She was perhaps one of those who wishes to say nothing . . . who has more than one reason for not living. . . . For years one may live next to someone who is no longer of this world."[14]

Anguish rises. A contrapuntal rhythmic effect is set up as the village folk, bearing the dead girl's body, slowly make their way toward the garden, following the "undulations of the path." The Old Man must speak out now. "One does not know in advance the march of pain."[15] He must inform the family. As the crowd approaches, the Old Man enters the house. Then, before he utters a word, the Mother walks forward. She has already understood the tragedy that has befallen her and hides her face in her hands. The Old Man nods slowly to the crowd, indicating he has completed his mission. The family rushes into the garden; the infant sleeps on.

Interior is an extraordinary work and an excoriating one. The inevitability of death is so powerful at times as to become unbearable. The contrast between the peaceful family scene, visible through the window, and the sorrowful news that must invade this atmosphere accelerates in intensity as the drama unfolds, reaching its apogee at the end. As in a classical drama, all unessential material has been eradicated; the play's theme (the obligation of informing the family) is always uppermost.

III   The Death of Tintagiles

The Death of Tintagiles is the last of Maeterlinck's dramas for marionettes. Here we are confronted with death in the form of a queen who dictates her inexorable blood wish and her maidservants who obey her will; thus showing once again man's impotence when dealing with destiny.

The young boy Tintagiles has been slated to die. His two sisters try to protect him from this fate. The queen, who has already destroyed most of Tintagiles's family, lives in a high and remote tower, the only area of the castle that has not been destroyed by time. Her servants are merciless in carrying out her will. They steal little Tintagiles while he sleeps between his sisters, Ygraine and Ballangère. Suddenly Ygraine awakens, realizes her brother is missing, and hurries to retrieve him. She enters a dark vault beneath the castle and hears a faint knock on the other side of a thick iron door. Her brother calls to her in a weak voice; he begs her to open the door and let him slip out, back to her. She strikes the door and claws at it, but her efforts are useless. On bended knees she cries out and begs the queen to free her little brother. When Ygraine hears Tintagiles's' tiny body fall to the ground, she screams out her rage: "Monster! Monster! I spit on you!"

Death as expressed in *The Death of Tintagiles* is no longer a spiritual force that perpetually hovers over man as was the case in *The Intruder, The Blind, The Seven Princesses, Pelléas and Mélisande,* and *Interior;* nor is death a senex figure who stealthily seeks out its victims. Death now has revealed itself, for the first time in Maeterlinck's dramas, in the form of a woman.

In many ancient mystery religions death was given the form of a woman, the giver and destroyer of life, the feeder of her creations and the devourer of her victims. The Terrible Mother Archetype represented in Babylonian, Assyrian and Indian statues is depicted as a devouring maw, a horrendous creature who annihilates and dismembers her victims. She is never satisfied; she demands and receives blood so that she may continue to live, creating and destroying.[16]

Maeterlinck had moved away from the strictly patriarchal situation, from the self-sacrificing child heroine. Dual forces are at work in *The Death of Tintagiles.* The Terrible Mother figure on the one hand and the positive sisters (Ygraine and Ballangère) on the other. Both aspects of the female principle are present and do battle throughout. Although Tintagiles's sisters fail, they nevertheless fight valiantly.

The Death of Tintagiles may be looked upon as a *rite de passage* not only with regard to Tintagiles's life-and-death drama, but also in terms of Maeterlinck the playwright. Although still deeply entrenched in Schopenhauer's philosophy (man has no power over his fate; his life is constantly subject to outer-worldly forces), the fact that active forces emerge in *The Death of Tintagiles* and battle with fate indicates the end of Maeterlinck's passive acceptance of life's forces.[17]

This play marked a turning point in Maeterlinck's theatrical style. He had descended into his depths — the darkened grottoes beneath the castle, the forests, the tenebrous gardens — he had completed his *rite de passage* and, unlike Tintagiles, was not caught behind the door but was capable of opening it at will. For Maeterlinck, the outer world was just coming into focus; slowly at first, then with increasing speed in the days and months that followed. Life was no longer simply a vale of tears. Joy, although always mitigated for Maeterlinck, was making its way into his world.

Maeterlinck was not only becoming a well-known playwright in France, his fame was also spreading to England. Shaw, Gosse, and Archer had written favorable comments on his work; many had read his plays in translation. When Maeterlinck arrived in London in March 1895 to attend the opening of *The Intruder* and *Pelléas and Mélisande*, he was greeted by ardent admirers and by a favorable press. An added delight was his meeting with W. B. Yeats and Harley Granville-Barker, whose talents were already well known to the Belgian playwright who had always admired English culture.

CHAPTER 4

Les Femmes Fortes

I. Aglavaine and Selyette — *A Death-dealing love*

ON January 11, 1895, Maeterlinck met the actress-singer Georgette Leblanc at a friend's home. She was an attractive woman; her blond hair fell in short ringlets about her oval face, creating a fitting background for her large eyes, straight nose, and sensual lips. Her manner was ingratiating, her personality dynamic. She was intelligent, well read, an interesting conversationalist who loved mystical subjects, and her approach to life and to art was sensitive. Maeterlinck was intrigued at first, then beguiled, and as the months wore on, the two became inseparable.[1]

Georgette's childhood had been unhappy. After her mother's early demise her Italian father, a shipowner, was given to periods of depression, creating a lugubrious home atmosphere. Compelled to rely on her inner resources for entertainment, Georgette became an avid reader of Montaigne, Plato, and Schopenhauer among others. The occult fascinated her. She sought out the Sâr Joséphin-Péladan, the founder of the Catholic order of the Rosicrucian sect. At seventeen she eloped with a handsome young Spaniard. He was a gambler about whom she knew little. Once again her life took on an ominous tone. Unable to obtain a divorce (there were no divorce laws in Spain), the couple separated. Depression ensued, and Georgette entered a sanatorium. When she became stronger emotionally, she started on a theatrical career. Throughout the troubled years her only source of pleasure was reading. It was through a book that she first became acquainted with Maeterlinck's works: his preface to I. Will's translation of seven of Emerson's *Essays*.[2] She fell in love with Maeterlinck, she recounts in her *Souvenirs*, after reading this book.

With Georgette as his constant companion, Maeterlinck was no

longer the victim of corroding despair; nor did he continue to find
mankind's lot so utterly without value. Not that Maeterlinck's
writings ever became jovial — not by any means. But a sense of
mitigated hope could be discerned as his life, for the first time, took
on a warm and peaceful tone. To add to his peace of mind was the
fact that he felt more secure in his career. His translations of John
Ford's 'Tis a Pity She's a Whore (1894) and Novalis's The Disciples
at Saïs (1895) won accolades from the critics.

Maeterlinck had been drawn to Ford, the last of the Elizabethan
dramatists, not only because of Ford's ability to express man's
fierceness, violence, lust, and abnormal passions, but also because of
the richness of his characters and the complexity of their natures.
Something of Ford's abnormal passions are present in Maeterlinck's
Aglavaine et Sélysette ("Aglavaine and Sélysette"), but in a
moderate form. Although this five-act drama has been called "a
canticle of mystical love,"[3] it would be more fitting to describe its
theme as love as an instrument of destruction. De Musset had also
dramatized a similar theme in his play One Does not Trifle with
Love, in which he stressed the negative outcome of such passion.

Structurally, Aglavaine and Sélysette is far inferior to
Maeterlinck's former works. It is prolix, repetitive, and lacks conci-
sion and originality. The insights are routine, the imagery ordinary.
What is of interest, however, is the nature of the love depicted: an
absolute, all-encompassing love that moves blindly, supposedly an
altruistic and positive force but actually an expression of egoism and
revenge.

Méléandre and Sélysette have been happily married for four
years. Sélysette is charming, childlike, and naïve. Méléandre enjoys
the open and frank nature of his wife. Aglavaine, the widow of
Sélysette's brother, announces by letter her forthcoming arrival.
Her love for them, she claims, is all-abounding. Because she has
known sorrow, she believes herself capable of great feeling and understanding. Although Méléandre has met her previously,
Aglavaine's arrival sweeps him off his feet. He believes in her quasi-
divine manner and the depth of her tenderness. He says it is
because of Aglavaine's affection for him that his feelings toward his
own wife have deepened. Sélysette's love for Aglavaine has
transformed her likewise: she develops increasingly celestial
characteristics. As time passes, Aglavaine's rapport with Méléandre

grows more intimate. Now Sélysette frequently regards herself as an intruder. She feels that her husband's love for her has diminished, whereas his passion for Aglavaine has increased. Sélysette goes to the tower and jumps off. Before she dies, Aglavaine and Méléandre implore her to confess to her suicide, thus relieving them of the burden of guilt. Steadfastly she maintains she fell while leaning over; it was an accident. Had she told them the truth, she believes, her sacrifice would have been useless. As a result, Aglavaine and Méléandre become tortured beings who can no longer love one another.

Aglavaine is one of Maeterlinck's most complex heroines. She is a negative matriarchal figure who hovers over the entire scene, a threatening force. Rather than spreading love, she divides, dismembers, and destroys. In some ways she is reminiscent of the queen in *The Death of Tintagiles*, more powerful here, perhaps, because of the deceptive love-disguise she wears. Aglavaine is convinced that she can love both husband and wife more deeply than they love each other, that her kind of love brings people closer: "We will put so much beauty into ourselves and our surroundings that there will be no room left for misfortune and sadness; and if these enter in spite of all, they must perforce become beautiful too before they dare knock at our door." The three, according to Aglavaine, are to experience a mystical bond; their union is to create harmony on earth and to enlarge upon life's enjoyment.

Artificiality intrudes upon the picture: Aglavaine's utterly repugnant attitude toward Sélysette and Méléandre as well as her doctrine of love. She is not the altruistic force she claims to be, nor are her unconscious desires fated to bring joy to others. Because of her self-delusion and her blindness toward the reality of her own being (and to life in general), she brings destruction. Aglavaine has really masked her true desires — those of revenge. Her marriage had not been happy and after her husband's death she felt rancor and dissatisfaction. The unhappiness she has known is buried under the guise of purity and love. Like a leech she begins to feed on others, to bestow her affection on the young couple, thus attempting to fill the void in her heart. Nor are her ways spiritual. The fact that she is constantly kissing Méléandre and Sélysette on the mouth at the slightest provocation indicates her need for physical contact, her intense desire for sexual fulfillment. Aglavaine resembles Lilith, a demon who brought destruction to her innocent victims. Sélysette and Méléandre are not wise enough to see through her.

Méléandre's love for Sélysette is based on joy and gay banter. Neither aspired to great heights. Satisfied with their earthly relationship, they frolic about. There is nothing profound in anything they do, in any of their thoughts. Theirs is a simple existence.

When Sélysette finds herself caught in a triangular situation, the only way she can alleviate her pain is by destroying the threesome. The question remains how to proceed. When she sees Aglavaine sleeping in a dangerous position near the edge of a reservoir, she could easily push her into the water. But she chooses to awaken her slowly and tenderly, thus preventing any accident. Sélysette is not yet ready to free herself, to commit that murder which would have ended her anguish.

Another matriarchal figure makes her presence known in *Aglavaine and Sélysette:* Méligrane, Sélysette's grandmother. She replaces the grandfathers of the earlier plays. Although always half asleep, unable to move from her chair, she is endowed with intuitive powers. She divines Sélysette's pain by her laughter; the unhappiness behind her smile. But Méligrane is too passive to intervene and therefore cannot function as a positive agent. She can merely feel the decaying state of affairs around her. Méligrane is a puppet figure; she cannot act, but is acted upon. She reflects the protagonists' feelings.

The tower from which Sélysette jumps is the focal point in *Aglavaine and Sélysette,* as the tower had been, but in a different way, in *The Death of Tintagiles.* The Queen of Death in the latter play made her plans high up in the tower. No one saw her, no one could communicate with her. Her decisions, carried out by her messengers, were irrevocable. In *Aglavaine and Sélysette* the situation changes. Sélysette chooses to direct her destiny, to take the situation in hand.

The fact that Sélysette opts for the tower as a means of solving her problem (a representative of heights and of spiritual attitudes) indicates her desire to return to the physical world, to become linked once again with early forces. Aglavaine had attempted to bring about a superhuman or overly spiritual state of affairs. When someone strives to reach such lofty heights, with a concommitant cutting off of earthly ties, a need to restore the balance ensues.

Aglavaine preaches the doctrine of brotherly love until it becomes a death weapon. In so doing she has adopted an extreme extroverted attitude, working on others rather than on herself.

A divergent drive takes place in Sélysette's personality. She who has been the extroverted individual, now, when faced with an unpleasant situation, becomes increasingly introverted and secretive in her thoughts and acts. No longer the open, happy, carefree childlike bride of the first act, she is transformed into an unpredictable and mysterious force as the play moves along.

Aglavaine sees the change in Sélysette. In Act III she expresses concern for her: "You must confess everything, as I confessed everything, my dear little Sélysette."[4] Why had Sélysette gone to the tower three times? she questions. Why had she leaned over so far when she knew how dangerous it was to do so? Sélysette tells her that a strange bird has been flying about the tower for the past five or six days, "an unknown bird with green wings, but of such a strange green and so pale. . . ."[5] No one knows where the bird came from. Sélysette wants to unravel the mystery of this celestial messenger. Aglavaine warns her to be careful. The previous night she had a nightmare in which the bird had played an active part. She begs Sélysette not to return to the tower.[6]

The bird image is in itself very interesting. The green of the bird usually represents hope and fecundity. In this particular image, however, the green takes on a strange tonality — as if endowed with some outer-worldly nature. As noted before, according to Egyptian hieroglyphics, the bird with a human head represents the soul, the Ba. The bird may therefore symbolize Sélysette's soul in projection. To understand the bird, its origin and wanderings, would be to understand Sélysette. The bird's departure would indicate the liberation of Sélysette's soul or her death. While using the bird as an excuse for her presence on the tower, Sélysette was in effect describing the steps pointing to her own demise.

Sélysette's suicide brings not love but anger to Méléandre: "And all my pain has been transformed into disgust!" He repudiates Aglavaine and her sinister love: "I spit on the beauty that has brought misfortune."[7] An unfortunate, guilt-ridden life is the price paid for an excessive and blind love.

When Georgette Leblanc read *Aglavaine and Sélysette*, she was disappointed. "He had wanted to create a heroine who would have pleased me, and this so-called "clairvoyant" woman exercised her strength without discernment on two beings who were incapable of understanding her. . . . I hated this Aglavaine to whom I gave life and for whom I had been responsible." Georgette also felt that Sélysette was a contrived protagonist and that her suicide was out of character. Sélysette could have simply left Aglavaine and Méléandre to their own destiny, she asserted.

Aglavaine and Sélysette failed as a play. It is drawn out, lags, and its repetitions are monotonous. Even Maeterlinck was aware of these deficiencies. But *Aglavaine and Sélysette* was an important work because it marked a turning point in his dramatic career. Maeterlinck was slipping away from Symbolism and entering into a new literary phase. Certainly he was feeling the influence of Georgette Leblanc's dynamic and vibrant personality.

II   Ariadne and Bluebeard — *The Feminist*

Whether Maeterlinck had until now refrained from entering into any prolonged love relationship to avoid the suffering that often accompanies such liaisons or to maintain his independence is open to conjecture. Georgette Leblanc put an end to this attitude. Scintillating, dynamic, witty, she had the strength and courage to face the exigencies of life from which Maeterlinck habitually shied away. Although twelve years his junior, she seemed to play the role of a mother figure to Maeterlinck. She protected him against everything he disliked: intrusions by reporters, over-zealous friends, the curious, and well-wishers. Maeterlinck must have been overwhelmed by such solicitude. In his diary he notes: "I cannot believe you are possible."[8]

There were other facets to Georgette's personality that were equally alluring to Maeterlinck. A cultured woman, she was familiar with the works of such mystics as Plotinus, St. Augustine, Boehme, Fénelon, and Mme Guyon. More important than the cerebral knowledge she gained from her readings was the empathy she felt for these beings. Her letters to Maeterlinck were replete with mystical terms: "I love you in what you term light . . . and if I were to be separated from you forever, I feel that I would continue to love you immutably."[9]

Theirs was a complete relationship: physical and metaphysical, giving Maeterlinck the strength to cut his ties with his family once and for all. Georgette was the catalyst. His decision was momentous, to be sure, but he knew that if he were to evolve as a playwright, he would have to leave his native city of Ghent and move to the freer, more creative atmosphere offered in Paris. Georgette looked upon it as "the natural work of love.[10] Maeterlinck had been dependent upon his family both economically and emotionally. Although liaisons were acceptable to the bourgeois society in which Maeterlinck lived, his own father having indulged in them frequently, to live openly with a theatrical star was more than his family could agree to. At the age of thirty-two, Maeterlinck rejected family structure and moved to Paris with Georgette.

They could not marry since she was still officially married to her Spanish husband and only the Pope could end that union. Moreover, Georgette was determined to maintain her independence. She did not want the ties of matrimony, so to live together for as long as love lasted seemed to her, and to Maeterlinck, the ideal solution.[11]

Georgette and Maeterlinck moved into a rather calm district in Paris — Passy, not far from the River Seine on rue Pergolèse. Maeterlinck's privacy was maintained and his quiet insured. Since he despised noises of all types, Georgette saw to it that the household help observed the rule of "silence." During mealtime, which Maeterlinck looked upon as a "sacred" period, no one was admitted to their home.

Though solitude and silence were *de rigueur*, neither Georgette nor Maeterlinck were recluses. They entertained quite frequently. Poets, writers, and artists were invited to their home but always at their convenience: Octave Mirbeau, Maurice Barrès, Jules Renard, Jean Lorrain, Colette, Paul Fort, Rachilde, Anatole France.[12]

The next several years could be called euphoria. Georgette and Maeterlinck spent their winters in Paris and their summers in a rented home in Normandy, which they called Montjoie. Frequently she went on tour or filled engagements, enhancing her own reputation whenever the occasion proved right. Maeterlinck published almost continuously during this period: a collection *Douze Chansons* ("Twelve Songs", 1896); essays, *Le Trésor des humbles* ("The Treasury of the Humble," 1896); *La Sagesse et la destinée*

("Wisdom and Destiny," 1898); *La Vie des abeilles* ("The Life of
the Bee," 1901); a play, *Ariane et Barbe-Bleue* ("Ariadne and
Bluebeard," 1902).

Maeterlinck's *Twelve Songs* consisted of poems based on
folksongs.[13] Like Gérard de Nerval and Paul Verlaine, Maeterlinck
had always delighted in immersing himself in the lyrical out-
pourings of popular tradition. He loved the earthiness and tender
spirituality of those who lived close to nature, who instinctively had
the ability to communicate with this transcendental force. The simple folk fascinated him: their love, their desolation, even their innate cruelty, as expressed in the stanzas and lulling refrains, taught
Maeterlinck much about the human character. Maeterlinck's poems
captured these qualities, focusing mainly on the soul and its continuous attempts to break out of the tenebrous world in which it was
held prisoner. Maeterlinck's *Twelve Songs* reflect his own dual
nature: his attraction to the spiritual, or Apollonian, side of life and
his need for the physical, or Dionysian, tendencies.

The essay form, perhaps even more than Maeterlinck's poems or
plays, enabled him, at least intellectually, to come to terms with
reality, a state of being he had always shunned. Like Montaigne,
Maeterlinck struggled to assess the forces of society and nature by
understanding philosophers: Plato, Plotinus, Marcus Aurelius,
Ruysbroeck, Boehme, and the more modern Novalis, Carlyle, and
Emerson. Like the Renaissance essayist, Maeterlinck used to jot
down his thoughts, sayings he had read, questions that bothered
him, then elaborate upon them to create his own credo. His inborn
pessimism, his deep sensuality, his longing for things spiritual, and
his rejection of organized religion were all food for contemplation,
filling the pages of his loosely constructed and discursive essays.

The Treasury of the Humble is metaphysical in nature. It begins
with a quotation from Thomas Carlyle, "Silence and Secrecy!" both
vital factors for Maeterlinck. "Great things" and "great thoughts,"
Materlinck believed, were formed not in chatter but in stillness:
virtue, the greatest of values, was born in secrecy. Both silence and
secrecy are essential to the well-being of the soul. Many individuals,
unfortunately, fear silence and the void that follows. "Most people
understand and permit silence to reign only two or three times in
their lives. They do not dare greet this impenetrable host except
during solemn occasions, but almost all of them, at this time, greet

it with dignity. Remember the day when you experience silence for the first time and without fear. The frightening hour resounded; and it came upon you preceding the advent of your soul."[14] It is in "true" silence that the soul finds its refuge, that communication with others on the profoundest levels of all becomes possible. "No sooner do the lips sleep than the soul awakens."[15] Gesture and facial movements allow the soul to evolve, to breathe its feelings and sensations in visual and perceptible form. To understand the world of the soul, an arcane domain that lives outside of the conscious sphere, is to comprehend that aspect within man which links him to the universal pleroma; it also permits him to comprehend the transition to be made from the amorphous (or uncreated) entity, bound by neither time nor special concepts, to the concrete work of art, experienced in the limited, finite world of the conscious mind.

To try to render the workings of the soul comprehensible to others (or to oneself) to translate them into verbal form (or temporal molds) is to falsify and to limit its capacities. Since language as we know it is an instrument of the cerebral mind, it no longer belongs to the atemporal realm of the soul; it no longer speaks in universal terms. The woman, Maeterlinck believes, is capable of transmuting the soul's message via sensations and feelings. She is a *mediatrix* through whom man discovers his own arcane realm, enabling him to express or exteriorize his own potential. The woman, writes Maeterlinck, "is ready, day and night, to respond to the highest exigencies of another soul,"[16] and because of her capacity to *feel*, she probes, insinuates, and experiences at a deeper level than man.

In Maeterlinck's essay *Wisdom and Destiny* one senses the powerful influence of Marcus Aurelius's stoicism as elaborated in his *Meditations*. This Roman emperor, whose reign was marked by war, famine, and disease, was a monist — that is, nature was *one* for him. He looked upon virtue as life's supreme value, a harmony with the divine forces (or nature). If one lives in accordance with nature, he asserted, evil becomes nonexistent. Neither death nor misfortune, therefore, are regarded as negative factors but occur in accordance with nature's cyclical pattern.

Eastern philosophical teachings, deeply rooted in a sense of fatalism, are discernible in *Wisdom and Destiny*. But Maeterlinck's version of karma was not completely fatalistic or passive. He had already moved away from Schopenhauerian negativism to a view tempered with Occidental optimism. It is possible, he intimates, for man to alter his destiny if he so wills. Man is double: he lives both an inner and an exterior existence. When developing the former domain, he taps his own inner resources, encourages them to flower and to strengthen, and in this manner he becomes, to a certain extent, master of his destiny. "The will to wisdom has the power to rectify everything that does not affect our body mortally."[17]

Marcus Aurelius succeeded in dominating his misfortunes through wisdom, through his capacity to reason, to accept, to understand both the negative and the positive aspects of worldly ways. Moreover, he believed that misfortune could in itself be a positive instrument. Pain and suffering encourage inner growth and strength; if man circumvents or tries to overcome these unpleasant sides of existence, he will develop his own powers.[18] An analogy may be drawn between Aurelius's discipline and the athlete who exercises and achieves mastery over his body.

Only by confronting life in its dual manifestation, its mystical and realistic aspects, he declared, can some semblance of happiness be experienced. "To be happy is to have transcended the desire to experience happiness." One must then be above and beyond the meaningless word "happiness." Felicity and peace are experienced within the individual, and are not like the result of worldly accomplishments which leave man a slave to hope and fear, unable to cope with these forces.[19]

Ironically enough (and one cannot help but recall Molière's satire on the stoic philosopher in his play *The Would-be Gentleman*), the philosophy which to a certain extent surfaces in *Wisdom and Destiny* should have endowed its author and his companion with a more reasonable and understanding attitude toward life, greater detachment from society's materialism, and more control over their hyperemotional temperaments. Instead, this essay caused a rift between them. Georgette insisted that *Wisdom and Destiny* should have been co-authored since it had really been a joint venture. For some time it had been their habit to jot down their spontaneous thoughts on pieces of paper and to stick these in a special area on a wall "like a butterfly." Maeterlinck would remove the papers every now and then and include the thoughts in his essay. Strictly speaking, therefore, *Wisdom and Destiny* was not solely his work. Yet he refused to accede to Georgette's wish. To settle the misunderstanding, Maeterlinck agreed to dedicate the volume to Georgette as follows: "I dedicate this book to you, which is so to speak your work. There is a higher and more real collaboration than that of the pen, it is that of example . . . . It was sufficient for me to listen to your words. It was sufficient for my eyes to follow you attentively in life; they followed the very movements, gestures, habits of wisdom." Although the altercation was peacefully settled, the cause of the misunderstanding stemmed from the vanity and egotism of two individuals. Therefore, one may say that despite the lofty ideals and great philosophical solutions to temporal and atemporal problems, man is — and certainly this is true of Maeterlinck and Georgette — made of loam.

Human nature was not the only aspect of life that fascinated Maeterlinck; he was also interested by the insect. In *The Life of the Bee*, which did not purport to be a scientific treatise yet was free from error, Maeterlinck drew parallels between the bee and man.

There are bees, asserted Maeterlinck, who appear to be doing nothing at all, yet they carry out a precise function essential to the well-being and evolution of the group. Likewise, there are thinkers in human society who ponder and weigh, who construct and formulate ideologies; but because they do not move about are the object of castigations aimed at them by the rabble who blindly conclude that the thinkers are lazy because they are physically immobile. The bee, also like man, is gregarious and cannot thrive in isolation; the individual is subservient to the group, abandons his freedom for the sake of the hive or the state. Maeterlinck reasons that bees, like man, have willpower and possess complex brains in which natural wisdom prevails. The bee, Maeterlinck further asserts, is also subject to mood changes. When, for example, the beekeeper collects the wax from the hive, he will not be stung if the bee, having fulfilled its function in life, is happy; so man reacts positively to situations when his potential is being developed.

During these productive years Maeterlinck did not remain in France continuously. He traveled briefly to Spain, Germany, Holland, and England. In June of 1898 he went to London to see Mrs. Patrick Campbell create the role of Mélisande. She had asked Gabriel Fauré, who was in London at the time, to write the "incidental music" for the play. The costumes, designed by Sir Edward Burne-Jones, one of Maeterlinck's favorite artists, were exquisite, particularly the gold dress worn by Mélisande.

Maeterlinck was delighted with the production. He wrote Mrs. Campbell his thoughts: "You have taught me that one need never be afraid of dreaming dreams of too great beauty, since it is our good fortune now and then to meet a privileged being who can render them visible and real."[20]

Pelléas and Mélisande was an "overwhelming success." As for Maeterlinck, he was hailed "the Belgian Shakespeare."[21]

Although Georgette saw to Maeterlinck's comforts and desires, she was in no way subservient to him; nor was she yielding. She was a woman with a career, determined to make her way as both singer and actress. Some of Maeterlinck's friends, among them Lugné-Poë, believed Maeterlinck was dominated by her, overwhelmed by her dynamic and vibrant personality. Pierre Descaves felt she brought out Maeterlinck's potential, the inner man always hidden from sight, banished from the light. Suppositions may be offered, guesses made — the enigma remains. Partial insights into Maeterlinck's inner world may be gleaned from a philosophical and psychological appraisal of his next play, *Ariadne and Bluebeard* (1901).

Bluebeard had always been a frightening yet enthralling character. His escapades were modeled on the famous fifteenth-century villain and murderer Gilles de Retz, Marshal of France, who had fought alongside Joan of Arc against the English. Gilles de Retz was an alchemist, a sorcerer who not only kidnaped beautiful women, but children as well, to be used in his multiple experiments and his satanic orgies. The seventeenth-century Charles Perrault based his tale *Bluebeard* on this evil being. He narrated the story of the wives Bluebeard had married and killed, and the last one who had been fortunate enough to escape alive. Maeterlinck's version, although dealing with the legendary figure, focuses on the character of the seventh wife, Ariadne, analyzing the stamina with which she faced her ordeal and emerged relatively unscathed.

The play opens as Bluebeard brings his bride Ariadne to his castle and gives her six silver keys and a gold one, with explicit instructions not to use the latter one. Ariadne opens the first six doors; as she does so, torrents of jewels fall into the floor. When she unlocks the seventh door, she hears the cries of women and discovers Bluebeard's previous wives. Bluebeard surprises Ariadne at work and locks her up with the other women beneath the castle. The peasants hear of Bluebeard's cruelty. They catch him, beat him and tie him up. Ariadne, who witnesses the struggle, sends the peasants away, then tends to her husband's wounds together with the other wives. Ariadne, however, decides it is time for her to leave and beckons the other wives to follow. They refuse, and remain with Bluebeard. Only Ariadne departs. To have bothered to free the other wives, she now realizes, had been a useless endeavor.

Maeterlinck's Ariadne is a woman who refuses to be dominated by anyone and who is capable of carving out her own destiny. "He loves me," she says about Bluebeard. "I am beautiful and I shall discover his secret." She lives according to her own rules and has a plan. "First one must disobey; that's the first step in overcoming a menacing and inexplicable order. The others were wrong, and if they are lost, it's because they hesitated."[22] Ariadne is direct, courageous, forthright. Like the Cretan Ariadne who gave Theseus the cord to guide him out of the labyrinth, thus enabling him to return to humanity, so Maeterlinck's Ariadne may also be associated with this ancient, forceful, leader-type female principle. It is not surprising that Maeterlinck's protagonist uses the golden key since she knows fully that "whatever is permitted teaches us nothing."[23] Only the hidden, the secret, the difficult, is worthy of human effort.

Ariadne's Nurse, who accompanies her throughout the play and is forever reacting emotionally to every situation, opens the various doors. A dazzling array of sapphires, diamonds, rubies, and other precious jewels stream onto the proscenium. The "irradiation" from the diamonds is so blinding, it is almost intolerable. In a lyrical apostrophe Ariadne personifies the diamond, this miraculous stone which for her has become a living substance: "Immortal dew of light! Streaming on my hand, illuminating my arms, dazzling my flesh! You are pure, indefatigable and you never sleep as the passion of clarity becomes agitated in our fires, like a people of spirits who plant stars."[24]

Because diamonds are resplendent and light, they are frequently associated with *gnosis;* and in this play with Ariadne's thirst for freedom and light. She is the light-bringer in Maeterlinck's drama since she has attempted to illuminate what was living in perpetual darkness and confusion — the other wives. She has the courage to venture forth alone in forbidden and, therefore, terrifying realms, which is the fate of many light-bringers.

The doors opened throughout the play are looked upon as feminine symbols since they are barriers that enclose a darkened, uteruslike area. The fact that a golden and not a silver key is used to penetrate the forbidden realm indicates that the riches therein contained are far more precious than those placed behind the other doors. The gold of the key stands for solar light, divine illumination — alchemical symbols for everything that is superior, pure, and spiritual. Through heightened intelligence or supreme illumination one may have access to the inner world and assess the riches therein. Ariadne knows that only clarity of the mind and independence of spirit can bring enlightenment and fulfillment. Each individual must seek these goals for himself so that what Aristotle termed *entelechy* may be experienced.

The wives imprisoned in the underground vault may, psychologically, symbolize Ariadne's own unconscious fears, the timorous aspects of her nature she tries to hide or reject and with which she is constantly at odds. Because Ariadne seeks to confront these forces buried within her, she exhibits the strength necessary to fight her battle against Bluebeard and win her independence.

After the peasants wound Bluebeard, she tells them to withdraw because he has done her no harm. She remains unafraid of him and has understood life's great lesson: the one who resorts to force and bloodshed to solve his difficulties is the weaker one. The other wives, shuddering in fear, are to be pitied. To them Ariadne says: "My poor, poor sisters! Why do you want to be delivered if you adore your darkness?"[25]

When in Act III Bluebeard returns, this time with his servants, and again is wounded by the peasants, he is cared for by his wives. Ariadne is the exception. She has learned her lesson. She beckons to her sisters, encourages them to emerge from their "tomb," their lifeless existence, to follow her to freedom, to light, to consciousness. "The moon and the stars illuminate all the roads . . . (and) reveal to us a world inundated with hope."[26]

The Cretan Ariadne led Theseus out of the labyrinth. Maeterlinck's heroine emerges alone from the darkness. The labyrinth in the original Greek version of Ariadne represents the world of instinct, confusion, and chaos, as does the underground vault in Bluebeard's castle. The twentieth-century heroine, like her ancient prototype, stands for the forces of reason and intelligence over those of fear and restriction. Bluebeard's wives were imprisoned because they did not merit freedom; invaded by fears, subservient in all ways with regard to their domineering and cruel husband, they likewise dreaded liberation and the world at large. Rather than opt for the unknown, the new and possibly the frightening, they preferred to suffer the brutality and pain of incarceration.

Ariadne and Bluebeard, though less compact and dense a work than *The Blind* or *The Intruder,* is nevertheless interesting from a philosophical point of view. It is one of the first dramatic analyses of the liberated woman. Unlike the bombastic and overly passionate romantic heroines featured in Victor Hugo's *Marion De Lorme* or Alexander Dumas's *The Lady of the Camellias,* or such cut and dried figures as depicted in Henry Becque's *La Parisienne,* Maeterlinck's Ariadne is vital and relevant for contemporary theatergoers.

Audiences and critics alike responded with praise to Maeterlinck's play. Despite Lugné-Poë's reservations about Georgette's talents as an actress, she brought success to the Théâtre de l'Oeuvre — on May 7, 1902.

III   Sister Beatrice — *A Liturgical Drama*

Maeterlinck had always been preoccupied with the question of fate. For the mystic who believes in a cyclical time scheme, divisions into past, present, and future are considered arbitrary, a view Maeterlinck shared. In his important essay *Le Temple enseveli* ("The Buried Temple"), (1902), he discusses his fluid concept of time and duration.

He asserts that for many the past is an unshakable, inalterable, fixed segment.[27] But the past is not stable, Maeterlinck claims, it works continuously on the present and therefore on future events. "In truth, the power of the past is of the heaviest import, it weighs on men; it draws them toward sadness." The past that lives within each individual is cumulative. It can be used, adapted, and transformed. As a living and breathing substance that acts and reacts upon individuals, it maintains a symbiotic relationship. The past, Maeterlinck continues, is enclosed within the memory and "there is nothing as variable and as impressionable, nothing less independent than this memory, which is forever enriched and worked on by our heart and our intelligence . . . ."[28]

Maeterlinck's views with regard to time resemble to some extent those of Henri Bergson as adumbrated in *Time* and *Free Will* (1899) and *Creative Evolution* (1906). Time, which Bergson thought of as a "rolling snowball" in that it is forever in a state of flux, continuously alters its consistency, and can be understood only through experience. It cannot be comprehended quantitatively, that is, in terms of the static, reversible time scheme as conceived by mathematicians. Maeterlinck likewise considered life a dynamic, growing, and evolving process that should not and must not be conceived in terms of static ideations. For both Bergson and Maeterlinck, memory is not merely a recreation of the past — events can never be relived in the same manner. The recollection of past events alters throughout life, affecting and working on an individual at all times. The past, then, is not subject to linear time but is part of that infinite entity known as duration or cyclical time.

Other similarities exist between Maeterlinck's and Bergson's ideations. Both men, for example, were intuitive types. In his works Maeterlinck did not proceed through cerebral analysis of the phenomenological world, but through something inexplicable that went beyond the comprehensible frame of existence and found its answer in universal harmony. "There is no art of composition in Maeterlinck's works," wrote Paul Flat, "rather there is a marvelous understanding of intimate notation, an art of sounding out the suffering soul and of perceiving within it the slightest quivering never before heard."[29]

In his *Introduction to Metaphysics* (1903), Bergson declares that intuitive knowledge is superior to analytical *gnosis:* the former being "absolute and perfect," the latter remaining "relative and imperfect." Reality, therefore is for the intuitive writer. a mobile and creative force that can never be reduced to static concepts even when concretized in the word. Each person reading a literary work or viewing a canvas projects his own unconscious onto the created bject and thus experiences it subjectively, altering it to suit his own needs.

Maeterlinck's writings, for example, are based on powerful impressions, themselves expressions of an inner climate. The prevailing sensations in most of his plays and essays are those of anguish and fear. "It seems that his characters live in perpetual anguish of that something which is going to decide their fate," wrote Paul Flat, "similar to those sick people who feel pain so acutely and who experience powerful hyperesthesia so that they react to an odor or sound which an ordinary person does not even notice."[30]

Fear and anguish predominate in Maeterlinck's three-act play *Sister Beatrice* (1902), a drama based on a medieval miracle play by the Benedictine monk Gautier de Coinci (1177—1236).

It must be recalled that the cult of the Virgin had become very popular in France during the twelfth and thirteenth centuries. This new focus resulted in part from the Crusades and the concomitant influence of Middle Eastern and Oriental religions in which the female figure played a powerful role. The Feast of the Immaculate Conception, for example, took three centuries to travel from East to West. It was celebrated in the Middle East from the eighth century on, but in England not until the eleventh.

St. Paul, the harbinger of patriarchal Christianity, had done his best to unseat matriarchal worship, as witnessed by his attitude toward Diana in Acts (19:24—28). As a result of the suppression of matriarchal deities, some strange Christian sects arose during the early centuries. The Collyridians in the fifth century A.D. worshipped the Virgin Mary in the same manner as the ancient Egyptians and Greeks had adored Isis and Diana. In early Christianity the cult of the Virgin had not yet been strongly integrated into church doctrine, and the miracles of the Virgin in medieval times and later history (e.g., Lourdes, Fatima) were individual expressions of an immense need among the people. The scant details offered in Biblical texts with regard to women were elaborated upon by monks and religious people during the Middle Ages ostensibly for propaganda and educational purposes. The many cathedrals and sanctuaries built during that period could thrive only if parishioners or pilgrims filled their halls; thus legends and tales grew around these places of worship, many of which were devoted to the Virgin.

Because of the emphasis placed on the patriarchal aspects of Christianity, the missing female element created a void in the hearts and minds of the devout. It had to be filled somehow. The extreme need Christians felt for the Female Principle became manifest in the twentieth century with the proclamation of the Assumption of the Virgin Mary as dogma.

Gautier de Coinci used the writings of the Latin author Hugues Farsit as source material for the fifty-four miracles he gathered together and narrated. His goal was to convert non-believers to the cult of the Virgin. Ironically, while preaching a doctrine of love, Gautier de Coinci dispensed hatred and violence because of his intolerance, particularly to Jews.

Sister Beatrice takes place in a convent near Louvain in the fourteenth century. A young nun has fallen in love with Prince Bellidor and plans to leave the convent with him. Before departing, she prays to the statue of the Virgin for guidance. Both Beatrice and the Virgin look exactly alike. Beatrice leaves. The statue comes to life, and the Virgin takes Beatrice's place in the convent. For twenty-five years she devotes her time to kind deeds. Then Beatrice returns to the convent sick and despairing. She confesses her sins to the nuns, and they refuse to believe her, so convinced are they that she had never left. Beatrice dies revered and loved. The Virgin stands on her pedestal once again.

The conflict dramatized in *Sister Beatrice* resides between spirit and flesh, celestial and terrestrial needs, inner and outer life. Bellidor represents life, excitement, and fulfillment. These human joys are the very ones Beatrice has been taught to overcome and reject, since the flesh is considered the sinful part of man. But rather than fight for lofty ideals, Beatrice yields to earthly physical love.

Maeterlinck shows Beatrice's inner transformation by external means. Bellidor removes her nun's vestments and dresses her in the magnificent robes and jewels he had brought with him. Garments represent the *persona* — the mask — that aspect of an individual he or she seeks to reveal to the world. After Bellidor has put these fineries on Beatrice, her entire countenance alters. The beauty and purity of her features, heretofore hidden behind heavy veils now becomes visible. These great veils, Bellidor exclaims, "are made for death and not for life."[31] The inner and outer person, once split, have now coalesced. The life of penury, humility, and sacrifice, which had not been to her liking, vanishes. Joy and ebullience take their place. "Here are the clothes of your life which is just beginning! I am not taking one of the Lord's slaves away, I am returning a sovereign to love!"[32] Even the Virgin's face, Bellidor remarks, shows no anger, on the contrary, "it pardons, it radiates."[33] Beatrice must experience worldly love in order to live life fully.

Maeterlinck had chosen two of the triurnal aspects of the Virgin Mary to dramatize in his play: the celestial figure, the mother of Christ; and the terrestrial woman, the mother of the other children she bore with Joseph. The statue represents the celestial Mary and Beatrice her earthly counterpart.

The Virgin is depicted in pastel tones: blond curls, white skin, purity of countenance, and bluish highlights in her dress. Beatrice is endowed with similar hues. "Look at her hair through which your hair shines as my hands part the quivering veil . . . . They are the same rays, emanating from the same light and the same source of joy,"[34] says Bellidor. Beatrice's face is bathed in an ethereal and spiritual light. For Bellidor the Virgin and Beatrice are one — an anima figure, aspects of the Great Mother archetype he must possess.

Maeterlinck unified what had been differentiated in the Magna Mater archetype: the terrestrial maiden (Beatrice) and the all-spiritual Virgin (Mary). This consolidation becomes concretized scenically when the Virgin steps down from her pedestal and dons Beatrice's veil and cloak. At this moment, the celestial Virgin gives way to her human earthbound side — the mystery has begun. Consequently, images endowed with both heavenly and earthly aspects are *de rigueur*. "Why did you infuse your dress with light?" questions a little girl who has just entered the convent, convinced she is talking to Sister Beatrice. "Why do stars appear in your eyes?" and "Why have you placed stars in your hands?"[35]

After the Virgin has taken Beatrice's place, the abbess notices the statue's disappearance and is aghast. The other nuns, equally stunned, observe that the one they believe to be Beatrice is wearing the Virgin's garments underneath her cloak. Fear envelops the religious community. Cries of sacrilege ring through the air. Beatrice has desecrated the statue of the Virgin. "Why sisters, my poor sisters! horror no longer has a name and our eyes have sounded out the depths of hell!"[36] they cry out. Virgin-Beatrice remains impassable. She is impervious to the condemnations heaped upon her, even when the nuns declare her to be possessed by the devil. The priest is called in. He encourages the sisters to treat Beatrice cruelly. They force her into the chapel. But no sooner does she enter the sacred area than sounds of "Maria Stella" fill the halls, "The nave is inundated with flames, and unknown splendors undulate about, flowering infinitely more dazzling than those of the sun whose rays illuminate the corridor."[37] A miracle has occurred and they believe that Beatrice has been sanctified.

With Beatrice's return the circle closes. Sick, haggard, and unrecognizable, Beatrice kneels before the statue of the Virgin as she had in Act 1. She begs pardon for her sins and is ready to die. The other nuns, now very old, rush in. They cannot understand the sudden change in Beatrice's features. She, whose face had never altered, whose beauty had remained fixed for those twenty-five years, has suddenly grown wrinkled and ill. When they look up and see that the statue of the Virgin is back in its place, they cry miracle. "The Virgin has returned! — She returns to us from Heaven! — She has brought her back to us!"[38]

Beatrice confesses her sins to the nuns, begs them not to nurse her, but to let her die. They refuse to believe her story. "You have performed only miracles, and you have been the light of our souls, the incense of our prayers, the door to prodigies, the source of grace."[39] But Beatrice seeks punishment for her misdeeds and not reverence. "I prefer to be outraged, I prefer to be harassed." The abbess tells her of the two miracles that have occurred. "The Virgin left us to return to Heaven; but before leaving she placed her sacred robe on you and adorned you with her crown of gold, her saintly ornaments, teaching us in this manner and with her infinite goodness that you would take her place during her absence."[40] Beatrice dies.

Georgette Leblanc, for whom Maeterlinck had written *Sister Beatrice*, won accolades for her portrayal. She embodied for the dramatist at this time in his life both the spiritual and terrestrial woman. Her understanding of the mystical side of life and her profound relationship with Maeterlinck in this sphere, as well as their physical union, seemed to unite what had formerly been divided within him.

With the creation of a single anima figure (in Beatrice and the Virgin Mary) the ideal and the real, the divine and the material were no longer antithetical factors, but worked in harmony with each other. The corrosively depressing dramas in which death had been the sole protagonist in a world drenched in nihilism seemed to have momentarily vanished.

IV   Monna Vanna — *The Political Heroine*

Maeterlinck's new dramatic style (represented by *Aglavaine and Sélysette, Ariadne and Bluebeard, Sister Beatrice*) opted for a combined philosophical-thesis play in which problems were posed and answered and characters were of flesh and blood. Gone were the lyrical dramas replete with spiritualized essences and mysterious, hermetic, arcane ideations. No longer were spectators able to penetrate a world of feeling and experience fluid language — varied sonorities that flowed in and out of a dialogue resembling prolonged litanies, melopoeias, and aubades. Non-objective scenery as used in the productions of *Pelléas and Mélisande, Interior,* and *The Intruder* (dim lights, moonshine, dark forests, grottoes, all creating an atmosphere of somber disillusionment) had vanished. Maeterlinck's world now was, for the most part, existential. Whereas his protagonists had heretofore succumbed to an all-powerful heimarmene, and were powerless in dealing with the hidden forces fate had sent to destroy them, he now had them act overtly. They participated in creating their future. Maeterlinck's earlier dramas had been spontaneous expressions of feelings, moods, and obsessions; his new brand of theatre would speak to the minds of spectators first — then, perhaps, to their feelings.

Certainly, the trends of his day must have made an impression upon Maeterlinck. More important, however, were the inroads Georgette's personality had impressed upon him. He was experiencing her not only as a force in his existential routine but also as a creative artist. The *femmes fortes* featured in his dramas from *Aglavaine and Sélysette* on were artistic transpositions of what he was living out in the real world. *Monna Vanna* (1902), Maeterlinck's new drama, was another manifestation of the Georgette-like woman — this time emerging as a political heroine.

Monna Vanna takes place in the fifteenth century. Pisa has been besieged by Prinzivalle, a Venetian mercenary who commands the Florentine forces. The inhabitants of the city are starving. Marco Colonna, the wise and understanding father of the Pisan commander, Guido, is sent to talk terms with the enemy. Prinzivalle wants to humiliate Guido. He therefore demands that Monna Vanna come to his camp and spend the night with him. Guido is outraged by such terms, but Monna Vanna understands the difficulties of the situation and is willing to sacrifice herself so that the multitude may eat. She spends the night with Prinzivalle, but he does not touch her. Instead, he declares his love for her which he has nurtured since he first met her when he was twelve years of age. With the coming of dawn, Prinzivalle is warned that his former Florentine enemies have surrounded the camp and intend to kill him. Monna, who now regards him as heroic and kind, is intent upon saving him and takes him back to Pisa. She tells Guido that Prinzivalle did not touch her. Her husband, however, does not believe her. He will have him killed. Monna in desperation lies and tells him that Prinzivalle had violated her and that she seeks her own revenge. Prinzivalle is put in prison and Monna is given the key. It is implied that Monna and Prinzivalle will escape together.

An analysis of *Monna Vanna* not only sheds light on Maeterlinck's own evolving relationship with the female principle, but also on his indecision with regard to literary problems.

The fact that the play features a conquered nation of Pisans, a people dying of starvation, reveals a certain psychological condition also present in *Pelléas and Mélisande*, a play written at a time when Maeterlinck had reached a literary and psychological turning point. When a nation is faced with sterility and destruction, it is an indication generally that something has gone amiss, that power has been lost and the creative instinct has vanished. A change must occur to awaken what has grown dormant and to replenish the void.

Sacrifice, which is the theme of *Monna Vanna*, is the catalyzing agent that may accomplish the needed transformation. Sacrifice, or martyrdom, a regenerative force, is part of all religions, from the most primitive to the most sophisticated. The sacrificing of tranquillity (status quo) destroys the prevailing stagnant orientation. Chaos ensues and with it fear for future well-being. New forces are thus brought to light, enabling the one affected to experience new insights, new perspectives. Prinzivalle is the external agent who paves the way for Monna Vanna's evolution, enabling her to transcend her circumscribed world.

The Pisan father, Marco, is a patriarchal figure. He and his son, Guido, are antipodal in nature. The wise and understanding father is sensitive to the ways of the world and sees what people need and want. He is the positive senex figure par excellence and for this reason is chosen to negotiate with the enemy. Because he is capable of visualizing the situation on a collective and objective level, he functions rationally at all times. Of course, it must be stated that he is not directly involved and therefore knows little conflict. He attempts to reason with his son: "you may ask if you have the right to deliver an entire people to death, to retard an inevitable evil for a few sad hours; because when the city will have been taken, Vanna will be delivered to the conqueror."[41]

Guido is not the pragmatist that his father is. His passion reigns and blinds him. Subjective in his views, he resembles a petulant child rather than a military leader. He is a man inflated with pride and belongs to the old school — when women were looked upon as possessions. Weakly structured, he is easily hurt and angered. When Monna decides to go to Prinzivalle's camp, Guido reacts personally. Rather than considering it a wise decision that would spare his people enormous suffering, he considers it a rejection of him.

Monna, a heroic and altruistic creature, examines the political situation from both a personal and impersonal viewpoint. Having made her decision, she feels her husband's pain so deeply, she cannot bear to look into his eyes. If she does, she will not have the necessary courage to fulfill her mission. Like a queen, she hides her anger and humiliation at being taken to Prinzivalle's tent. There she speaks to him in restrained and collected tones, Not once does she permit her anger or resentment to overwhelm her. Monna is worthy of admiration and Prinzivalle accords her her due.

The themes of women hostages and rape have been dramatized from time immemorial Abduction and acts of rape are facts of history and the subject of many legends: the rape of the Sabines by Romulus's men, women captives taken after the Trojan War (Andromache, Cassandra), the rape of Europa and of Persephone. In so-called civilized societies, armies frequently rape the victims of beleaguered cities; in marriages of convenience a girl is symbolically sold to a man, indicating a kind of rape-sacrifice situation. Such acts are an expression of man's need to reveal his superiority over women or his unconscious fear of being a victim of overwhelming matriarchal forces. Rape is a way of proving sexual virility for some, a release of libido for others, the building of a fantasy life for an adolescent. It is an archaic way of thinking.

In Maeterlinck's play, however, Prinzivalle is not a rapist; on the contrary, and much to the audience's surprise, he becomes a superhuman hero. Pure in heart, gentle, loving, and courageous, he resembles those wise figures of ancient days in whom one had confidence. He is Marco's youthful counterpart. In endearing terms Prinzivalle recounts the incidents surrounding his first meeting with Monna Vanna in a garden in Venice when she was eight and he was twelve. It was then, he tells her, that he fell in love with her. Even when he was obliged to follow his father to Africa and thoughout all his trials — taken prisoner by the Arabs, Turks, and Spaniards — her image remained with him. Although Prinzivalle's adventures are incredible and are so exaggerated as to be worthy of Candide's outlandish plights, it is not as a soldier that he wins Monna Vanna's love but rather in his human aspect: his ability to be forthright, communicative, and always at ease with her.

Because of the very authentic feelings Prinzivalle arouses in Monna Vanna, she becomes aware of the superficiality in her relationship with her husband. She and Guido have nothing in common. Grateful to him for having married her when she became an orphan and impoverished, her affection has been based on appreciation and gratitude, not on a communion of souls. Moreover she has never really loved her husband viscerally. Without emotional and physical rapport a *whole* relationship cannot be built; it is forever lopsided. Guido must have been aware of this state of affairs. He must have realized that his passion for his wife remained unreciprocated. Having no faith in the depth of her love for him, he fears her departure and considers her sacrifice a betrayal of him rather than an expression of altruistic feelings for the community at large.

Monna Vanna is indeed a queenly figure. She uses her judging faculties, reasons out her situations, and acts with heart. She is greeted upon her return to Pisa with a heroine's welcome. "The mothers extend their arms so that she would touch their children; and the men lie on the ground kissing the stones on which her feet have brushed."[42] Her victory would have been complete had her husband believed in her story. Her attitude toward him, until now docile and submissive, turns to anger. His refusal to believe her compels her to resort to deceit to save the situation. Only Marco understands the significance of her lie. Once a forthright, open, loving wife, she has to be dishonest to become an authentic individual — to live life fully for the first time. Only now does her true identity emerge, giving her the strength to end a relationship that has grown sterile and destructive. Her sacrifice altered a peripheral and conventional existence. Real life to be lived with Prinzivalle — though hazardous — is now to begin, one based on a rapport between two independent human beings respectful of each other.

Maeterlinck succeeded in proving certain philosophical concepts in *Monna Vanna:* the sacrifice of an individual (a wife's purity in this case) is valid to save a multitude; superficial relationships cannot stand the chaos of upheaval and only authentic rapports are valid.

The critic Emmanuel Arène of the *Figaro* (May 18, 1902) responded to Maeterlinck's new brand of semirealistic, semithesis theatre. He enjoyed Georgette Leblanc's interpretation of the heroine: she "admirably incarnated the noble and beautiful Vanna." He praised Lugné-Poë's direction that brought out the "truth and startling melancholy" of the events depicted and the characters portrayed. Maurice Beaubourg of *La Plume* (June 1, 1902) was far from impressed with Maeterlinck's new venture. As for Maeterlinck's old friend Charles Van Lerberghe, he too considered *Monna Vanna* inferior to Maeterlinck's previous works.[43]

Maeterlinck did not overly react to the songs of praise or condemnation leveled at *Monna Vanna.* Respected, wealthy, successful, loved, he seemed to have found a new way and was certain to pursue this course. When in 1903 the Belgian government awarded him the Triennial Prize for Dramatic Literature, he accepted it with pleasure, so convinced was he that it was merited.

V   Joyzelle — *An Initiation*

Joyzelle, Maeterlinck's next play, is clothed in fantasy; however it deals with the very real problems of building a durable love relationship. Adversities encountered and overcome in life may be thought of as successfully completed initiations. Those ordeals serve to strengthen individuals and enable them to gain insight into themselves and others. Rather than embarking blindly in a series of adventures or romantic escapades, a higher force will be called into play, permitting the participants to make a sharp and lucid choice before all undertakings.

Joyzelle takes audiences back to the medieval world of Merlin the magician, that ancient senex figure endowed with clairvoyance and

the power of prophecy. Although Maeterlinck's protagonist is infinitely more accessible to the modern psyche than Geoffrey of
Monmouth's Merlin, he is, nevertheless, also imbued with strange
spiritual powers.

Merlin has fascinated countless generations. Marvels surround his
name. It is said that he had been instrumental in moving the huge
stones from Ireland to Stonehenge in England; that he had once
been an ancient Druid priest; that his kindness and perversity had
stemmed from the fact that his father was believed to be a devil and
his mother a pure maiden. He had worked in conjunction with the
Fates when he saw to it that Uther Pendragon inseminated Ingraine
who then gave birth to King Arthur. Wace's *Roman de Brut* (1155)
and Malory's *Morte d'Arthur* (1485) depicted Merlin as a wise old
man who paved the way for King Arthur's greatness. At the end of
his long life, it is said, Merlin succumbed to his passion for the
sorceress Vivien and finally became her victim.[44]

Maeterlinck's play takes place on a bleak, enchanted island ruled
by Merlin. The fairy Arielle, his only companion, is invisible to
everyone but to the magician. Joyzelle, a beautiful maiden, arrives
on the island in a thick fog, and Merlin falls in love with her. According to certain prognostications, if Merlin's passion for her is
repressed, he will die. Then Lancéor, Merlin's long-lost son, is
washed ashore and he too falls in love with Joyzelle. Lancéor and
Joyzelle must undergo rigorous tests, or initiations, if their love is to
be fulfilled. Although Merlin is fully aware that his life will end
once his son's passion is reciprocated, he helps the young couple
overcome their ordeals and enjoys the thought of their happy
destiny.

The most arresting features in *Joyzelle* are found in the psychology of the characters of Merlin and Arielle and in the initiation
ritual Lancéor and Joyzelle must undergo in order to be free to
unite in love.

Merlin is a *complexio oppositorium:* he is devilish and kind,
physical and spiritual, shortsighted and visionary. Endowed with
prophetic gifts, he is privy to both past and future events; but he
has lost sight of the immediate situation and does not know how to
cope with existential problems confronting him.

His situation, as the play unfolds, has become critical. A price
must be paid for Merlin's gnosis; that is, the overevaluation of the

intellectual sphere and the sacrifice of the world of instinct. Merlin thus far lives only in the domain of the mind, as is the case of "highly civilized" man. Merlin's rational forces have been developed to the extreme and at the expense of his feelings. He speaks the language of flowers, birds, and trees, and is in this sense an animist, but he cannot cope with the human element. The only inhabitants on the island are servants who pass by in silence. The fact that Merlin can communicate with trees, flowers, and birds — entities belonging to other spheres — indicates yielding his intellect to instinct — and a concomitant merging with the *unus mundus*, a phase of existence he must experience if he is to heal the split between instinct and intellect.[45]

It is significant that Merlin's only companion on the island is the fairy Arielle. The word *ariel* in Hebrew means "lion of God," the animal who was said to have been an aide to the prophet Ezra. The lion has frequently been alluded to as a "subterranean sun," or inner fire, indicating latent passions within a human being. Merlin, perhaps for this reason, described Arielle as "my inner strength, the forgotten power which lies dormant in every soul," or instinct.

Arielle is Merlin's *anima* figure, an aspect in projection of his ideal woman, of his undervalued instinctual realm. She describes herself as an appendage, cut off from Merlin like "a fantom lost in the night." Her loneliness is intense at times. "I do not belong to myself, I obey my master, I have nothing to give but an invisible kiss."[46] Because Merlin experiences her unconciously, he does not understand her needs and her lionlike nature. She represents a problem to him: she is unpredictable, undependable, and has the personality of a trickster, a sprite. The more uncontrollable her behavior, the greater is Merlin's antagonism toward her and the more troublesome she becomes.

It is Arielle who will pave the way for Merlin's enlightenment. She helps him to become cognizant of his son's needs and the split within himself. As an instinctual being, she lives close to nature and has learned its secrets. She shares these at times with Merlin. She informs him of his son's plight: "He thinks himself lost; and his destiny leads him to happiness which awaits . . . . Destiny must be decided freely and a father's love, of which he is completely unaware, must not ruin the test . . . . Your son's destiny is inscribed in a circle of love."[47] From Arielle Merlin also learns the importance of the instinctual world from which he had been cut off for so long. "Instinct alone will save man,"[48] she claims. Only when harmony exists between the thinking and feeling functions will life be lived fully.[49]

The first indication of Merlin's desire to experience wholeness rather than conflict occurs when he withdraws to an island. To cut oneself off from people does not necessarily indicate a desire to escape. It can also reveal a need for *introversion*, the digging deep within oneself in order to better understand the hidden dichotomy. When he learns of Lancéor's passion for Joyzelle, the anguish he feels between both facets of his personality comes into play for the first time. Heretofore he had been unaware of his son's needs, a fact which was symbolically expressed by Lancéor's disappearance. Lancéor's coming to the island signifies the emergence of Merlin's feelings and his need to relate to his son (or what he represents in Merlin's psyche). Once Merlin experiences the chaos that comes from the turmoil, a reappraisal of his activities occurs; instinct and intellect fall into place when he accepts nature's way: the young must marry the young.

Maeterlinck's Merlin is fascinating because he depicts the plight of modern man who seeks to live life fully but is unable to do so. Cut off from the world of instinct, intensely preoccupied with his mechanized routine, he lives strictly in the sphere of the mind. Because so little attention is paid to the instinctual realm, it emerges abruptly, often destructively, sometimes engenders so much intensity that the form it takes cannot be coped with. Because of Arielle's persistence, Merlin listens to her advice, to the lessons of his "invisible daughter, the good fairy of the island,"[50] and becomes aware of the irreparable damage he could have wrought before it is too late.

What Arielle has taught, Pascal had expressed in the seventeenth century: "The heart has its reasons that reason knoweth not." When the intellect cannot solve a problem, let the natural man, or instinct, speak forth.

The initiation rites dramatized in Joyzelle, which Lancéor and his future bride must undergo, are of psychological interest.

Initiations have been part of religion since the Isis mystery rites in Egypt and the Eleusinian mysteries in Greece. They are intended to put man in contact with his own nature and experience, "the impersonal principle which really rules in the depths of his psyche."[51]

It is during the frequently harrowing initiation ritual that the individual faces his instinctual self and is made aware of his limitations. Because initiations usher in new frames of reference and new attitudes, they have been linked symbolically to death.

The ordeal, or test, "is designed to bring the initiate into direct touch with the deeper layers of the unconscious,"[52] thus enabling him to know himself honestly. Once he is made aware, he will be subservient to no one: neither to instinct nor intellect, neither to an anima figure nor his own shadow or any negative characteristics. In the Grail legend, for example, the postulant had to ask a question; in other ordeals, he was compelled to fight a battle. Whether the initiate follows one prescribed dictate or another makes little difference. In accomplishing his task he must unravel the mystery of his own identity, his role and function in life. If he fails to ask a question or to fight a battle, he remains unconscious of the deeper meanings of his activities and therefore is not qualified to go on to the next phase of psychological or spiritual development.[53]

Both Joyzelle and Lancéor arrive on Merlin's island by chance and in a deep fog. As such we may say in psychological terms that both are unconscious of their direction, activities, and destiny. Lancéor states he did not even know he was nearing Merlin's island. "Suddenly, without any reason, great bluish vapors invaded the waves. They rose like a veil which attached itself to the hands, to the rigging, to the face."[54] After the boat has docked and "the fog has lifted," he falls asleep in a grotto.

Lancéor, then, is totally unaware of his focus in life and of his identity. He is like a child bobbing up and down on the sea. "Several days ago I called myself Lancéor, I knew where I was and I knew myself. Today I am looking for myself, I grope around within myself and all about me."[55] If he were to pursue this rudderless life, he would never become aware of his existential plight, never earn independence and enter into maturity. Hurdles must be confronted and difficulties overcome if one seeks to pass from one phase of development to another. These obstacles may be regarded as initiation rituals.

Joyzelle, too, is in need of the initiatory process. Her ideations are blurred; thick fog had surrounded her entry onto the island. In fact, she had been destined to go elsewhere and to marry a young man her mother had chosen for her. Her unwillingness to adhere to such a plan indicates revolt on her part, a will of her own, an ability to achieve independence. But before she is able to find her own direction in life, she will have to pass through a chaotic state and face ever-present dangers.[56]

The first phase of the initiation process occurs when Merlin becomes aware of Lancéor's and Joyzelle's love. He threatens to destroy them both: "If I learn that you have seen each other again, you are irrevocably lost."[57] If they are to earn independence, Lancéor and Joyzelle must fight Merlin's interdict.

It is meaningful that their forbidden meeting should take place in a garden. But Maeterlinck's garden is the reverse of the Garden of Eden. In Genesis, the Garden is beautiful and peaceful. Maeterlinck's garden is dark and ugly: "The sun no longer comes there; the flowers have withered, the grass has shriveled, the leaves are sick, the old trees are dying, the springtime itself and the dew of dawn are fearful of being in this solitude."[58]

The young couple feels neither peace nor harmony, rather, fear and terror. Joyzelle begs Lancéor to withdraw, to obey Merlin. He refuses, and in this sense his disobedience may be considered heroic. "I have crossed the hurdle I had assigned to myself; I have disobeyed; and I want him to see it, I want him to know it."[59] The greater Joyzelle's fear, the more formidable is Lancéor's strength.[60] He refuses to yield to Joyzelle's fears and demands she open the door to the garden: "I look at the sky and the garden awakens:"[61] No sooner does she comply with his wishes than a transfiguration occurs. What had been disfigured and ugly has now grown radiant and beautiful. The trees are green, the flowers sturdy and colorful; the butterflies and the bees play in the sun.

Before Lancéor's heroic act, or the completion of his initiation, the garden symbolized sterility and death. To live without love, or Eros, is to divest oneself of life; to live under interdicts is to smother one's nature; to fear the senex figure is tantamount to castration. Such would have been the young couple's fate had they been incapable of undergoing the initiation ritual. Once they have overcome the constrictions, emotions can flow freely and develop, paving the way for a coalescing of disparate forces, thus insuring the course of life.

The young couple's ordeal is not yet over. While in the garden Lancéor was bitten by a snake, which Joyzelle maintains was really a "horrible animal." Merlin, now aware of his son's attitude toward him, decrees that Joyzelle must sacrifice herself if Lancéor is to survive. She is ordered to yield to Merlin. As Arielle maintains: "Man's weaknesses are frequently necessary in life's designs . . . . It is a question as to whether Joyzelle's love will overcome the test."[62]

Monna Vanna had resorted to deception to win her point, Joyzelle does likewise. She pretends willingness to sacrifice herself; but using a ruse, enters Merlin's bedroom while he sleeps. She takes out her little knife to murder him, thus ridding herself of her problem rather than confronting it. Arielle stops her hand in midair, saving her from irrevocable guilt. When the magician becomes aware of what has happened, he is shaken, then becomes cognizant of the young couple's determination to fulfill their destiny. Joyzelle and Lancéor not only bring about their own union, but symbolically, are catalyzing agents which bring about Merlin's own *prise de conscience*. His own higher awareness is the "goal of initiation . . . from the beginnings of puberty to the religious mysteries . . . . In all of them the higher spiritual man is begotten."[63]

It is significant that both Joyzelle and Lancéor arrived on the island from the element of water, primeval waters. Water has always been associated with the unconscious, the *fons et origo*. Since the couple emerge from water, they can be thought of as potential aspects or projections within Merlin's own unconscious. They are, then, transitional characters, creative forces, invisible and unproductive until they have been activated and rise to the surface of consciousness. They symbolize what Merlin lacks, Eros, or the capacity to relate in a harmonious manner. By their ebullience and vitality they show Merlin the way to joyfullness that is born when making others happy.

Joyzelle, produced on May 20, 1903, and featuring Georgette Leblanc, failed to impress audiences. Spectators remained untouched. The abstract notions and ideals, the philosophical implications of this drama seemed too remote, too far-reaching to elicit empathy from onlookers. In a fast-changing, mechanized, and industrial society, Merlin and the world of mystery and magic he represented had little significance for them. And yet these audiences should have listened to Maeterlinck's message; they might have been warned of the dangers awaiting them.

The lack of popular success did not affect Maeterlinck. He wrote a two-act comedy shortly thereafter, *Le Miracle de Saint-Antoine* ("The Miracle of St. Anthony"). A rather slight farce, it satirized man's credibility, his materialism, and destructive attitude toward the mysteries of nature. It, too, was unsuccessful when performed in Geneva and Brussels (1903).

Maeterlinck was not one to withdraw in the face of failure. A political mystery followed, *Le Malheur passe* ("The Cloud That Lifted"). Influenced by Ibsen and Strindberg, he thought, he too, would be capable of writing a dramatic study of jealousy. Maeterlinck, however, was incapable of dealing with such a complex topic realistically. As a result his protagonists are stilted, contrived, and superficial and their love-hate relationships are of little significance.

Clearly, Maeterlinck had reached an impasse. Once again he turned to the essay, *Le Double Jardin* ("The Double Garden"), to sound out his thoughts and converse with his inner world.

There are two gardens in life, Maeterlinck maintains in *The Double Garden:* one filled with beauty, sunshine, and joy; the other filled with menacing and haunting things which spread terror into the hearts of those who traverse it.[64] Man must, Maeterlinck asserts, attempt to uncover the enigma of his existence on both a personal and collective level.[65] In order to discover the *prima materia* of life, he should not remain asleep, "surrounded with darkness and the formidable silence of night."[66] Sleep has its function, is indicated in *Joyzelle* when the young people are brought to the island, but if a somnolent condition prevails, there is stasis. The world must be confronted in a waking state, and, though difficulties arise, they must be dealt with overtly. It is via the double garden that individuals learn to relate to reality, both inward and outward.[67]

CHAPTER 5

The Philosopher, the Mystic, and the Psychometrician

I   The Blue Bird

THE death of Maeterlinck's father on October 4, 1904, did not create a void in the dramatist's heart. They never had had a close relationship. Although father and son had felt an affinity toward nature, their views differed greatly as far as a writing career was concerned. Maeterlinck's father had always considered literature a supreme waste of time, a problematical and unstable career, and he expressed his opinions most openly. It was almost an irony of destiny that he could not be part of one of his son's greatest theatrical success — *L'Oiseau bleu* ("The Blue Bird").

The Blue Bird was written in Maeterlinck's home at Gruchet in Normandy during the summer of 1905. Maeterlinck had been approached by the editor of a newspaper who had asked him to write a Christmas story.[1] The play's theme was inspired, it has been claimed, by Mme Aulnoy's fairy tales, which Maeterlinck had read as a child, and by Grimm's stories as well as Perrault's *Tales of Mother Goose*. Most important, however, was J. M. Barrie's *Peter Pan*, the story of a young boy who ran away to never-never land because he did not want to grow up. Maeterlinck acknowledged Barrie's influence when he visited him in London in December 1909,[2] where he wrote on the wallpaper above the mantelpiece in the living room, "With my deep admiration to Peter Pan's father, the Blue Bird's grandfather."[3]

The Blue Bird's six acts and twelve tableaux center around the dream of two children: Tyltyl and Mytyl. One evening after they are put to bed, a fairy by the name of Berylune enters. She is old, hunchbacked, ugly, and resembles their neighbor Berlingot, whose daughter is crippled by illness. The fairy tells them to get dressed and go out of the window in search of the Blue Bird, which they are to bring back to her little girl who would "like to be happy." Berylune gives them a magic hat adorned with a diamond. If they turn the diamond around, the children are told they will see "the very essence of things" — the souls of Bread, Wine, Pepper, and others. Tyltyl turns the diamond and everything changes in appearance. The old fairy is transformed into a beautiful princess; the cabin becomes a dazzling palace. The fairy informs them that they will dine with their dead grandparents and brothers and sisters in the Land of Memory. The children's happiness is great as they embrace their beloved relatives. Then the children enter the Palace of the Night, The Realm of the Forest, the Garden of Happiness, and the Kingdom of the Future. However, they are unable to capture the Blue Bird before returning home. When they awaken the following morning, the children see everything in a different light. They are happier and their house is more beautiful. But when they tell their mother of their journey, she says it was only a dream. Tyltyl decides to give his own bird, which has now turned blue, to Mme Berlingot's daughter. The girl is so happy that her illness seems to disappear and she can walk again. She visits Tyltyl with the bird and asks him how to feed it. As he takes the bird to show her (perhaps with a bit of regret for his generosity), the bird escapes. The little girl sobs and Tyltyl tries to calm her. He asks the audience to help him find the Blue Bird.

The Blue Bird dramatizes a creation myth. A child usually symbolizes the reawakening force within oneself, the yet unformed contents within the unconscious; aspects of which are still moving toward their fulfillment before life closes its doors to change. Tyltyl and Mytyl are a pair of opposites who work in harmony with each other. They dream the same dream but experience it differently. Both emerge from the experience equipped to face the unexpected and difficult situations in life.

The first figure the children encounter in their fantasy world is the fairy Berylune, who looks like their neighbor Berlingot. The names are significant. Berlingot means burned sugar or caramel: she is sweet and suffering. Berylune is more esoteric; it is a composite word: beryl is a mineral, a crystal that may be found in a variety of colors, ranging from rose, yellow, and blue to green. In medieval times the crystal beryl was used to make magic mirrors that served for divinatory purposes. The combination of *beryl* (found within the earth) and *lune* ("moon") in the fairy's name indicates a hard, beautiful, and long-living substance allied to the more feminine, volatile, softer, and multifaced satellite inhabiting the heavens. Because of the complexity of the fairy's nature (stone and moon, matter and spirit), she stands for the various psychological values implicit in the play's peripeteia.

The ugly fairy is hunchbacked, lame, one-eyed. She is the human counterpart to the celestial fairy. She leads an unhappy life because of her deformity. Her daughter is also marred since she cannot walk. Something in the ugly fairy's life is unbalanced. Ugliness and sickness according to Paracelsus result from an unconscious inability to live in harmony with nature.

Whether ugly or beautiful is not the question; it is the function the fairy fulfills in the play that is important. She is a psychopomp, as Virgil was for Dante. It is she who leads the children out of their constricted world and permits their fantasies to flow freely; equips them with a magic hat and diamond to arouse their imagination. Like the primitives, the child lives in unison with nature; therefore anything is possible. Civilized man with his overpowering rational outlook is cut off from nature and cannot venture forth in the fantasy world.

The hat is of utmost significance. It draws attention to the head and to the mind. As a protective cover, the hat permits an idea to take root, unmolested by outside forces.

The diamond — a stone that has gone through a transformatory process within the earth to become crystallized carbon — is a luminous entity that stands for enlightenment. The children must turn it around in order to gain insight. For the alchemist the diamond signifies the completion of the first two stages in the purification process: from the blackness of chaos to orderliness and enlightenment. The diamond's function, then, is to illuminate. It endows Tyltyl and Mytyl with vision and they see into the "soul", or heart of things. They no longer rely exclusively on their human faculties — that is, the cerebral way of the adult. "All stones are the same, all stones are precious," Berylune tells them, "but man sees only some of them."[4]

Like the mystic and the alchemist, the children see nature as a living organism that breathes, sees, and feels. They react to their environment not as individuals separated from the metaphysical universe, but completely within its folds.

The fact that the fairy tells the children to leave their house by the window and not by the door, is also important. The bedroom door would lead to another part of the house before they got outside — a withdrawal before an exteriorization. The door has always played an important role in Maeterlinck's symbology (*Ariadne and Bluebeard*), as have windows (*The Intruder*). Both are apertures, ways of escaping from confining situations, the means of traveling through spatial spheres. Because the window is located above the ground, it encompasses more celestial domains; whereas the door, set on the ground, is linked to terrestrial activities. Hence, the children must fly above the pedestrian into more spiritual climes.

The first stop is the magnificent palace of the beautiful princess. Here the children meet their future companions: Dog, Cat, Sugar, Fire, Bread, Water, Light, and Milk. All these are personified by human actors; each is endowed with anthropomorphic characteristics. The Dog is man's best friend, his companion and slave, and is given human traits: faithful and kind. The Cat, in contrast, is egotistical, hypocritical, unpredictable, and is man's enemy. Sugar makes the children's journey more palatable.

The Land of Memory is the children's second stop. They meet their dead grandparents, brothers, and sisters in an atmosphere of diffused lighting. They hug them, rejoice with them, and sit down to a family repast. The communion of spirit permits a close rapport between the living and the dead. In such a plane, transfiguration takes place through memory: the children experience their past in the same form they had lived it. Here aging does not take place and death is meaningless. The grandmother and the others who have passed into another world, "are much better off since they are no longer alive . . . . There is nothing more to fear; one is never sick; one has no more worries."[5]

What does the Land of Memory signify metaphysically and psychologically? Analogies may be made between Maeterlinck's concepts in *The Blue Bird* and the beliefs of the Neoplatonists and Renaissance philosophers Kepler, Nicholas de Cusa, Giordano Bruno, and other philosophers such as Pascal, Leibnitz and Swedenborg. They believed the universe is a living entity filled with souls that are linked to one another, each an emanation of the totality of the universe. The manner in which the various souls act and counteract is governed by universal sympathy, the implication being that nothing is isolated in the cosmos and that everything has a cause and an effect.

Maeterlinck was becoming more and more preoccupied with the study of theosophy. He was familiar with the works of Helena Blavatsky (1831—91), *Isis Unveiled* (1887) and *The Secret Doctrine* (1888). She believed that dead spirits can be contacted. Their powers are not diminished when they pass on to the next world; their influence upon the living still prevails. Mme Blavatsky was also convinced that God can be experienced by individuals and that His secrets (those of the universe) have been divined by certain initiates: Buddha, Confucius, Zoroaster, Mani, Pythagoras, Moses, Christ, and others. The secrets known to the initiates have been and still are guarded by the "Great White Fraternity," a group of semiphysical and semiastral souls who enter physical bodies whenever situations on earth need rectifying. There is, Blavatsky maintained, a continuous telepathic rapport between earthly creatures and the souls of the departed who are forever looking out for mankind's welfare. The belief in the Akasic Record, an Eastern doctrine, was also incorporated into her credo. It affirms that everything that happens on earth as well as in man's mind is indelibly recorded on the Akasa, a form of ether that is believed to encircle the world. According to the visionaries of the Renaissance, if man disciplines himself in the practice of clairvoyance and meditation for many years, he will then be equipped to perceive, through Astral Light, certain signs within the Akasic Record and thus will be able to conquer or overcome death.[6]

Certain theosophic theories expounded by Mme Blavatsky are evident in *The Blue Bird:* that death is not an end to life but rather a transitional phase; and that communication exists between the living and the dead. The grandmother in *The Blue Bird*, for example, tells the children: "Well, each time you think of us, we awaken and we see you again."[7] Victor Hugo also revitalized these theosophic concepts in his poem *Olympio's Sadness*. He wrote that beings live as long as the memory of them remains in those still walking the earth. But Maeterlinck goes further than Hugo, he claims that the world of the dead is a replica of the world of the living: that having passed into transition, nothing changes, no evolution or devolution takes place.

That death is a mirror image of life in all its joyous aspects would be to believe in the myth of heaven. To claim that a static condition prevails in this celestial abode, that change is nonexistent, is to long for the continuation of an infantile fantasy. When children believe in such ideations, it is perfectly natural since their ego is undeveloped and they are still an intrinsic part of the cosmos — that is, there is no separation between subject and object. If a mature person believes in such stasis, it may indicate a state of psychological regression, an inability to accept the rigors of the world and the conflicts they entail. It is interesting to note in this connection that adult audiences were profoundly stirred by *The Blue Bird* whereas children took Tyltyl's and Mytyl's peregrinations as a matter of course.

The Palace of the Night is fascinating because of the austere, sepulchral, and metallic quality of the decor: an ancient Egyptian or Greek temple adding religious flavor to the atmosphere. Its most arresting feature is the character Night, represented by a female figure dressed in black. A negative quality is attached to Night and becomes obvious when we learn that the Cat, her friend, warns her of the children's desire to acquire the Blue Bird. Night must prevent the children from carrying out their mission. To capture the Blue Bird would mean to learn the secrets of the universe. "What do they want?" Night asks. "Must they learn everything? . . . [Man] has already seized a third of my Mysteries; my Terrors are fearful, they no longer dare to go out."[8] Night will do anything to prevent her secrets from being revealed. Once understood, she would be divested of her power. "I have kept all the secrets of Nature," Night informs the children, "and I am responsible for them; it is absolutely forbidden to give them to anyone, especially to children."[9]

Psychologically, Night may be equated with the unconscious. Within her possession are infinite riches and it is only through her that they can be discovered. Night, therefore, must never release her powers; once she does, the inaccessible, invisible world will no longer be a source of excitement and creativity.

Tyltyl is heroic. He demands that the doors to the various caverns be opened: those harboring sickness, catastrophes, mysteries, stars, planets, microbes, wars, and so on. Tyltyl investigates them all. He learns that man is no longer fearful of disease since microbes have been discovered; the specters do not cause anguish any more because "man no longer takes them seriously;"[10] and that wars are still dangerous. As they leave the Palace of the Night, the children grab as many blue birds as possible. But as soon as the birds enter the domain of light and air they wither and die.

What does the Blue Bird represent that the children search for it so intensely? It may be equated with the alchemist's philosopher's stone: a personification of the self, a *coniunctio oppositorum*. Within its depths the self contains the secrets of the universe and therefore represents wholeness and totality. Birds have always been associated with intuitive knowledge, with spirits and angels, with the higher aspects of life (thought, mind), and with celestial spheres. Since Cro-Magnon times birds have been soul images and soul bearers. Christ has been pictured holding a bird in his hand; St. Francis of Assisi is frequently portrayed talking to birds.[11] Because birds ascend, alchemists considered them activating forces in the sublimation process; paving the way for purity. The blue coloring of Maeterlinck's bird underscores the celestial aspect of the quest.

Night's great enemy is Light, who is the force guiding the children toward the Blue Bird. It is Light who betrays Night, who sides with man. Light is equated with *gnosis* or wisdom; it attempts to disperse the mystery of night, to do away with fear-producing powers. But Light, who encourages the rational or thinking process, is under no illusions. She knows that the real Blue Bird is very difficult, if not impossible, to find, and that it is hard to distinguish it from the multitude of blue birds flying around in Night's realm: "The only one which can live in the clarity of daylight is hidden here, among the other blue birds."[12]

The question remains why there is only *one* Blue Bird and why it withers in the light of day. Since the real Blue Bird, like the philosopher's stone, symbolizes the self, it may not be experienced in a differentiated manner, that is, in the fragmented realm of rational thought. Once Light shines upon it or discernment is used to understand it, it is no longer *one* but many. The Blue Bird is experienced only in the world of fantasy, in the unconscious, or in a dream. The children thought they had captured it but had taken the wrong one: "They were unable to attain it, it stood too high."[13]

Nature's secrets, it is averred, will never be revealed, not even to children.

Light continues to guide Tyltyl and Mytyl to the Realm of the Forest where trees have been growing since the beginning of time. At first the trees are happy to converse with the little strangers, but suddenly they regard them as enemies. Man has destroyed trees, they cry, he has cut them down. "The children we see here, thanks to a talisman, have stolen the powers of the Earth and can acquire the Blue Bird, extract from us the secrets we have been keeping since the origin of life . . . . Now, we know man sufficiently well not to have any doubt as to the destiny he reserves for us once he finds himself in possession of the secret."[14] The Forest is angered at the thought of man's hubris. The trees begin fighting with the children; but Light intervenes at the critical moment and informs the children of the dangers awaiting them when she is not there. Nature is very dangerous when one is unable to cope with it; therefore it is wiser not to stir up trouble.

Trees stand for both the existential domain (because their roots grow deep into the earth) and the spiritual realm (because of their verticality). They grow in darkness (forest), implying mystery and live for many years, representing nature's eternal aspect. Because trees grow upright, they have been likened to man (head, arms, legs, torso) and here are imbued with human personality traits (wise, patient); thus, when the children approach them, they become volatile and uncontrollable. Rather than attempting to understand the mystery of the trees in an analytical manner (a process too abstract for children), Tyltyl and Mytyl confront them in an arrogant fashion, arousing hostility and anger. Unable to cope with the forces unleashed by the trees (or within them if the tree is considered as an archetypal image), the children would have been engulfed by them had Light (reason) not led them to safety.

One of the most touching scenes in *The Blue Bird* takes place in the Garden of Happiness. Here life's goals are analyzed: the wrong ones (gluttony, ignorance, materialism, vanity) and the right ones (working, thinking, understanding, loving). The most beautiful love of all, Maeterlinck implies, is maternal love which can be extended to include a feeling of love for all mankind. Such love brings the highest and most intense form of happiness: "All mothers are rich when they love their children . . . . There are no poor ones, there are no old ones . . . . Their love is always the most beautiful of joys . . . . And when they seem sad, a kiss, received or given, is sufficient to transform all their tears into stars.''[15]

In the Kingdom of the Future the children visit the unborn, those who will one day journey to earth. The inclusion of the world to come gives *The Blue Bird* a cyclical dimension, a feeling of continuous cosmic life as experienced in the various spheres of our existence.

When at the end of the play Tyltyl's bird escapes, it is an indication that the childrens' fantasy life is over; the real struggle in the existing world is now to begin. The little girl has been cured, owing to Tyltyl's act of kindness. Happiness, however, is not stable; it must be earned, it cannot be given. Since life is an ever-changing process, nothing remains fixed — neither joy nor sorrow. Whatever is to be achieved will come as the result of an individual's fortitude and courage. Tyltyl is young and vital; he has confidence in life and will struggle to attain his potential.

Audiences the world over reacted enthusiastically to *The Blue Bird*. First produced at the Moscow Art Theatre (September 30, 1909), under the direction of Stanislavski, then in London the following year and on March 2, 1911, in Paris, at the Théâtre Réjane, it won astonishing notices. Nevertheless, there were some dissident voices, W. B. Yeats in particular, who felt Maeterlinck was merely at the services of Georgette Leblanc and had attempted, theatrically speaking, something beyond his capacities.[16] Maurice Boissard (April 1, 1911, *Mercure de France*), however, heaped praises upon the play and on Georgette's portrayal of Light: "Her voice, her attitudes, her gestures were harmonious."

Meanwhile Maeterlinck relaxed in the south of France in his new villa "Quatre Chemins" in Grasse (1906), a white house overlooking the Mediterranean. It offered him the seclusion he longed for and the esthetic contentment necessary to his art. Georgette, however, did not welcome the purchase of the house at Grasse. Her theatrical commitments did not permit her long stays there. But the lengthy separations between them did not seem to bother Maeterlinck.

He spent his idle hours meditating, writing, or immersing himself directly in nature: its shrubs, trees, and insect world. He expressed the intensity of his emotions in panegyrics to the wonders and mysteries of nature in *L'Intelligence des fleurs* ("The Intelligence of Flowers," 1906).

For Maeterlinck, nature was not merely an object of study, but a way of communing with a collective entity, a living substance. He felt revitalized by the touch of a flower, the chirp of a bird, the solidity of trees. Like the Romantics, he considered nature a companion upon whom he could project all his anguishes.

The question of immortality also came under Maeterlinck's scrutiny in *The Intelligence of Flowers*. Just as the mystics Plotinus, Boehme, and Ruybsroeck were convinced that nothing dies in the cosmos but is transformed, so Maeterlinck reiterated: "As is true of everything which exists, so we are imperishable."[17] Every change is transformed in an ascending pattern; therefore a higher morality will emerge from man's earthly struggles. Since life is eternal, Maeterlinck asserted, what could be the nature of anterior existence? Could past be felt in some way in this world? Could a new intelligence be awakened within the individual that would permit him to transcend the phenomenological world? Maeterlinck's thoughts were turning inward; clearly, he was preoccupied with metaphysical questions.

He broached a multitude of subjects, nevertheless, in *The Intelligence of Flowers*, including politics. He advocated a socialist doctrine and even wondered whether a bloody revolution with all of its evils would not be preferable to the agony of generations who experience perpetual injustice.[18] But Maeterlinck's political attachments were for the most part philosophical arguments and abstract idealizations. He did not divest himself economically of his worldly goods to help the poor, nor did he participate in any revolutionary groups. He did, however, contribute some money to various unions and socialistic groups.

During the years 1906 and 1907 Maeterlinck wrote little, and the few things he did conceive were of poor quality. His play *Marie-Victoire* (1907), a vehicle for Georgette, dramatized the plight of a woman who tries to protect her aristocratic husband from the brutalities of the revolutionaries. Even Maeterlinck admitted the play was inferior.

His heart was evidently not in playwriting. He was feeling more and more removed from the workaday world. A re-evaluation of his life's attitude must have been the goal of his meditations. Perhaps the inward flow of his energies prevented him from expressing his ideas verbally.

The death of his old friend Charles Van Lerberghe in 1906 added to his depressed state. New surroundings might help overcome his despondency. Heretofore, Maeterlinck had spent his summers in Gruchet Saint-Siméon. But its many trees, large gardens, and shaded porch were no longer conducive to his relaxation and creativity. Maeterlinck decided to rent the fourteenth-century Benedictine Abbey of St. Wandrille in Normandy. Its grandeur, history and spaciousness intrigued him. Georgette, attempting to re-create the medieval atmosphere this magnificent cloister called for, frequently donned the mantle of an abbess. Maeterlinck, a rather practical man at heart, put on roller skates when he wanted to go from one hall to another.[19]

Despite the new surroundings, Maeterlinck's literary vein was withering. Georgette noticed a kind of passivity and a disinterest for things intellectual. He spent his time fishing, gardening, meditating. She interpreted his indifference to all but his natural surroundings as a commentary on their relationship and became concerned. When Maeterlinck first met her, she claimed, he was going through his "first turning point," now a second phase of his existence was coming to pass.[20]

II *Neurasthenia*

Maeterlinck's inertia continued. Nothing seemed to interest him. His doctor diagnosed the condition as "neurasthenia," the result of nervous exhaustion stemming from some unconscious emotional conflict. No real cure existed for his ailment except a long rest from all intellectual work. The doctor suggested that Maeterlinck relax and empty his mind of all anxiety-provoking thoughts.[21]

It took months of relative idleness before Maeterlinck's interest in anything theatrical was rekindled. It happened quite unexpectedly. He was reading Paul Heyse's *Maria Magdalene* and had been deeply moved by the protagonist's courage. Maeterlinck wrote to the German author and suggested he adapt the play for French audiences. He also informed him of his willingness to share all profits with him. Heyse rejected the entire project. Maeterlinck then set to work on his own version of Mary Magdalene's dramatic life.

Maeterlinck's three-act drama *Mary Magdalene* focuses on the steps leading to her conversion to the teachings of Jesus and her reaction to His crucifixion. A beautiful and fascinating courtesan, in love with and loved by Verus, a Roman military tribune, she enjoys happiness and prosperity. Upon hearing of Jesus's miracle — the resurrection of Lazarus — she comes to worship Him. Verus, unable to understand her change of heart, believes she has fallen in love with Jesus. His jealousy is unbounding. When Mary discovers that Verus can save Jesus from crucifixion, she goes to her lover and pleads for His life. Verus agrees to pardon Jesus providing she give herself to him. Maria refuses. To do so would be to betray her honor and Jesus's words. Thus Maria permits Jesus's crucifixion. Her act, according to some, is sublime — an indication of the highest form of love.

Mary Magdalene is a drama devoid of inspiration. The characters are contrived, flat, and uninteresting, particularly Mary. There is nothing credible about her, neither her beauty nor sensuality as a courtesan, nor her sudden spirituality and sense of sacrifice in her devotion to Jesus. One has the distinct impression that Maeterlinck wrote this play as a vehicle for Georgette's tempestuous nature.

Maeterlinck's Mary bears little resemblance to the New Testament figure, referred to frequently as "the harlot," who became one of Jesus's followers and "out of whom he cast seven devils."[22] Maeterlinck's protagonist is a hysteric who enunciates platitude after platitude in bombastic and inflated language.

In Act I she parades in a stunning outfit on stage: a purple mantle embroidered with glittering stones, in sharp contrast to the pink tones of her dress. She greets Verus whom she has not seen in a while in angry terms; she reprimands him for comparing her beauty and his love for her to Solomon's ideal woman — the Shulamite. She hates Biblical texts. As for the Jews, they are dirty and ugly hypocrites, she maintains. Her hatred is so forceful and emerges in such powerful tirades that one wonders how such a virago could inspire love in anyone. Nevertheless, Verus adores her. No sooner said than Mary bursts forth in another torrent of anger; she has been robbed of her pearls, rubies, and — worst of all — a precious vase that dates back to Solomon's time. To have castigated Solomon and his society, then to regret the loss of a vase that is a product of his civilization makes little sense.

Incredible as it may seem, Mary, who has given herself to many men for material gain, has not yielded to the one man who really loves her, Verus. Indeed, she talks to him openly of her trade. She is far from being ashamed of her prostitute ways; on the contrary, with experience she has become more skillful; she gloats because she sells herself for more money than before.[23]

Mary's passion rages throughout the drama, from hatred, lust, and material gain to masochism in her extreme spirituality. She reacts emotionally when told that Simon has been cured of leprosy and Lazarus raised from the dead. Her posture is so extreme when she is drawn to Jesus as if by some incredible outward force that she gives the impression of moving more like a robot than a convert.[24] Her ways are stiff, her demeanor stilted; the entire sequence looks contrived.

Jesus's followers look upon Mary as a sinful creature and begin stoning her. Verus, watching the entire procedure, brandishes his sword to defend her. Christ, however, makes one gesture and one statement and all the activity ceases. "Let he who is without sin cast the first stone!"[25]

There is only one character of interest in the drama, Silenius, a friend of Verus and a disciple of Seneca. Silenius quotes the credo of the stoics, who preach freedom from passion and desire, detachment from material possessions, and overcoming the fear of death. Like Seneca, he believes in man's ethical progress that will come with a higher type of moral conduct. Virtue is life's goal, he claims. Knowledge is the sole instrument able to overcome adversity. To preach such a lofty point of view is indeed praiseworthy; but as is usually the case with such idealists, they never live up to their preachings. Silenius, supposedly above petty passions such as hatred, indulges in deprecating remarks aimed mainly against the people of the Holy Land. But he is also a moderating force in the drama and for this reason may be looked upon — in contrast to the others — as calm, controlled, honorable, and living in relative harmony with himself.

In Act II Mary becomes aware of her evil ways. She confesses her negative characteristics to Verus. "I felt the evil, the cruelty, and the despair which live in my heart . . . . But now, you can see, I am no longer the same person. I no longer know myself because I have found myself."[26] She has had a change of heart, she informs

Verus. Yet her personality remains the same. She is as demanding, as extreme as before. She wants him to take her away from this land she despises. Verus agrees. In the course of their conversation, he happens to mention that he has received orders to arrest Jesus and His most important disciples. Mary, in typical hysterical fashion, has a sudden change of mood. She is terrified and reminds Verus that it was Jesus who had saved her from being stoned. As she talks about Jesus, she feels elevated: "I felt that joy was invading my soul, like a kind of light which engulfed my thoughts . . . . He stared into my eyes but only a fleeting second, and this will suffice for the rest of my life."[27] Mary's sudden and quixotic ways are so exaggerated as to inject a farcelike character into the scene.

The most incredible — and laughable — sequence occurs when Lazarus walks on stage. He is pale, naturally, since he has been dead for four days. He walks like a zombie and is described "as something which has not yet become human again." He speaks to Mary: "Come, the Master is calling you."[28] She walks toward him as in a "somnambulistic trance," as if guided by the strings of destiny.[29] Verus, attempting to stop her, backs away, convinced this entire scene was planned to pave the way for Mary's departure with Jesus.

In Act III, Mary's passion (just as extreme as in earlier scenes) is now totally geared to self-abnegation and penitence. She is dressed in rags and knows only excruciating sorrow. "She is crazy with pain," Martha (Lazarus' sister) asserts. "She screamed, tore her clothes, and hit her head against the wall of Hanan's palace." No romantic heroine, no matter how outlandish her fury — neither Hugo's Marion Delorme nor his Doña Sol — could have expressed her grief in more extravagant terms than Mary. Because Mary refuses to yield to Verus, although it would mean Jesus's release from crucifixion, she now believes she has risen above earthly entanglements. She has accepted Jesus's fate, she claims. Her sacrifice complies physically and spiritually with His credo of divine love.

Maeterlinck's *Mary Magdalene* lacks the intensity and lyrical beauty of *Sister Beatrice*. So overstated is Mary's passion — on worldly or spiritual level — that her sacrifice at the finale seems more an act of masochism, of mental derangement, than a religiously motivated one. Mary is a woman so riddled with hatred, antagonism, and animosity at the outset of the play, so repulsively aggressive after her conversion, that the doctrine of brotherly love preached by Jesus does not seem to have altered her disposition one iota.

Like Edmond Rostand's religious work, *The Woman of Samaria*, Maeterlinck's drama is worn and dated. The characters are neither symbolic nor realistic, neither natural nor ethereal. Although the dialectics of Stoicism and Christianity are underscored in the drama, both views stressing the spiritual side of life and reviling the flesh, it is done in an almost grotesque fashion: the dichotomy between the characters' words and their comportment is too vast.

Although *Mary Magdalene* was written in 1908, it was not performed until 1910 in Leipzig and 1913 in France.[30] The critics were not enthusiastic. Clearly, Georgette Leblanc, for whom Maeterlinck had written *Mary Magdalene*, was no longer an inspiration to him.

III   *The Unknown Host*

August 28, 1909, may be looked upon as an event in theatrical history. A fervent admirer of Shakespeare in his youth, Maeterlinck had taken it upon himself to translate *Macbeth*. Georgette had the genial idea of producing this work in their newly acquired residence, the fourteenth-century abbey of St. Wandrille in Normandy. The spacious halls, the stark rectory, and the columned walks increased the reality of Shakespeare's work, thus enhancing its excitement for contemporary spectators.

Only sixty guests at a performance were permitted to buy tickets, costing two hundred francs each. By keeping audiences to a minimum, Maeterlinck and Georgette felt, the impact of the spectacle would be greatly sharpened.

Opening night was unforgettable. The moon sparkled. The large metal containers of burning hot coals that had been placed in various parts on the grounds and the monastery itself cast eerie lights and shadows over the entire area. Notables invited to the performance were greeted by the actresses and actors already attired in their costumes.

The action throughout the performance moved from hall to hall, from inside the abbey to outer areas, and the spectators followed. Such a mobile production impressed the audiences, who found it more authentic and searing. Gaston Calmette, editor of the *Figaro*, Princess Murat, Adolphe Brisson, R. McKenna, the First Lord of the Admiralty were agreeably surprised by the venture — or adventure. Rarely, if ever, had plays during the nineteenth century been performed out of doors, and with such abandon and yet such density.

The response from the critics in general was so favorable that Georgette was encouraged to produce other works at St. Wandrille. The following summer, 1910, it was *Pelléas and Mélisande*. Sacha Guitry and Réjane, among others, were present at this performance and had only words of praise to utter after their return to Paris.

Maeterlinck was growing increasingly annoyed. The success of the productions at St. Wandrille was encroaching upon his privacy. He could not tolerate such a state of affairs. To keep the peace, Georgette had to abandon her plans for future productions at the abbey, notably *Hamlet* and *Princess Maleine*.

Trips to London, Ghent, and the south of France did not help him dispel another bout with depression. The grief he suffered at his mother's death on June 11, 1910, added to his despondency. Although Maeterlinck had not seen her too frequently since he moved to France, he had always been deeply attached to her. He never forgot that she had had faith in his literary projects from the beginning and that she had lent him the money necessary to make his first publishing venture possible.[31]

Maeterlinck's life pursued an even course, but for some strange reason it seemed empty. There was nothing new in the offing. He had become increasingly detached from Georgette. There seemed to be no way to alleviate his pessimism. Trips, rehearsals, and solitude seemed to follow each other in quick succession and were becoming an inevitable routine.

During a rehearsal of *The Blue Bird* at the Théâtre Réjane, Maeterlinck was impressed by an eighteen-year-old girl who played two minor roles in the drama — Renée Dahon. She came up to him to ask for his autograph. The simplicity of her ways and her candor and beauty shook him quite visibly. The daughter of a wealthy merchant, she represented all he lacked at this juncture in his life: youth, optimism, joy.

Renée Dahon became Maeterlinck's cheerful companion and life took on a joyful note again. Gone were the lugubrious pessimism, the dreariness and apathy of preceding months. Maeterlinck decided not to settle in Grasse during the winter months because of the cold climate. He bought the "Villa Ibrahim" on the Colline des Baumettes just above Nice and renamed it "Villa des Abeilles." There, with a view of the Mediterranean, a garden filled with eucalyptus and fruit trees, Maeterlinck spent the next ten years of his life.[32]

The fact that Maeterlinck won the Nobel Prize for Literature might also have contributed to his new-found sense of buoyancy. The citation given him read as follows.

To Maurice Maeterlinck, on account of his diverse literary activity and especially his dramatic works, which are outstanding for their richness of imagination and for poetic realism, which sometimes in the dim form of the play of legend display a deep intimacy of feeling, and also in a mysterious way appeal to the reader's sentiment and sense of foreboding.[33]

Other honors were to accrue to Maeterlinck, among them the Grand Officer of the Order of Leopold. Some of Maeterlinck's friends could not understand why he accepted the award from the Belgian monarch, thus supporting a government he disliked, and a church he considered anathema, regressive, authoritarian, and intransigent. By 1913 Maeterlinck was expressing his socialist views openly. In the spring of that year, when the Belgian trade unions declared a general strike, Maeterlinck sided with the labor movement against the Catholic party, and offered the editor of the Brussels newspaper *Le Peuple* an essay on the subject.[34] To the leader of the strike, he sent a check for one thousand francs.

Maeterlinck's close friends Grégoire Le Roy and Van Lerberghe felt bitter about his fame. Grégoire, whom Maeterlinck had known longest, had not even been invited to the reception in Brussels honoring Maeterlinck. Many compatriots and Frenchmen considered Maeterlinck self-centered and egotistical, always preoccupied with his physical comforts, his needs, and his world.

Maeterlinck was either oblivious to the criticisms voiced by former friends and admirers or he was indifferent. Except for short trips to Paris, Brussels, and sometimes London, he remained in his villa in Nice. He indulged in some of his passions: boxing and motor-cycling, but mostly spent his time in meditation, reading, and writing. He became more preoccupied with the mystical side of life. Cosmic existence seemed to engulf his every thought. His essay *La Mort* ("Death"), written in 1911, was really an inquiry into the meaning of life.[35]

Maeterlinck rejected the pat answers to life and death offered by various religions, specifically Roman Catholicism. He was convinced of the eternal nature of universal consciousness. He did not, however, believe in metempsychosis or reincarnation, which are part of the Neoplatonist credo. Though his notion of universal consciousness was vague, he felt that the state after earthly life would be a relatively happy one. Like Descartes, he could not conceive of an eternal life in which despair would be the central core. There had to be something else.

The Catholic Church declared that the ideas advanced in *Death* were not only unorthodox but also destructive. *Death* was placed on the Index. When the newspaper *Le Soir* asked Maeterlinck for his reaction to the censure, he replied with a telegram: "Did not know of excellent piece of news. Publisher will be delighted. For the rest, prehistoric phenomenon of no importance."[36]

In the preface Maeterlinck wrote to J. H. Fabre's volume *The Life of the Spider* (1910), one notes an increasing interest in extra- or outer-worldly phenomena. "The insect does not belong to our world," writes Maeterlinck. "The other animals, even the plant, notwithstanding their dumb life and the great secrets which they cherish, do not seem wholly foreign to us."[37] There is something bizarre, mysterious, unfathomable about insects, suggests Maeterlinck. "One would be inclined to say that the insect comes from another planet, more monstrous, more energetic, more insane, more atrocious, more infernal than our own. One would think that it was born of some comet that had lost its course and died demented in space."[38]

In his essay *Our Eternity*, Maeterlinck asserts that man muses persistently on questions of death. "The more our thoughts struggle to turn away from it, the closer do they press around it."[39] Man should be allowed to delve into the notion of death without being labeled negative or depressive. Moreover, death is a natural course of events. Life should not be prolonged by doctors who feel obliged to keep those who are mortally ill alive and in pain. Doctors in such cases become torturers.

For Maeterlinck there are four solutions to questions of survival after death: total annihilation, survival with consciousness, survival without any kind of consciousness or survival in the universal consciousness (a consciousness which differs from any we can conceive).

Maeterlinck vetoes the first possibility. He did not believe in total annihilation. "We are prisoners of an infinity without outlet, wherein nothing perishes, wherein everything is dispersed, but nothing is lost."[40] The survival of an individual consciousness did not appeal to him either. "Would our body be conscious of itself without our mind? . . . What would our mind be without our body? We know bodies without mind, but no mind without a body."[41] Yet any notion of immortality bears the mark of individual identity. The Catholic Church guarantees, Maeterlinck declares ironically, that the "earthly ego" not only is preserved, but the flesh is resurrected.[42] He argues logically when he states that if one believes in a future existence, then one must believe that one has always existed; yet there seemingly is no consciousness of any previous existences.[43] He questions the validity of such an attitude. Maeterlinck assumes that there is a kind of universal consciousness or at least a modified consciousness in which all creatures are encompassed.

Belief in reincarnation is the most plausible answer with regard to the afterlife. The "doctrine that the soul in its successive existences is purified and exalted with more or less rapidity according to its efforts and desires is . . . the only one that satisfies the irresistible instinct of justice."[44] Such a concept is far superior, writes Maeterlinck, than the "barbaric Heaven and the monstrous Hell of the Christians, where rewards and punishments are forever meted out to virtues and vices, which are for the most part puerile, unavoidable, or accidental." But, Maeterlinck adds, the argument for reincarnation is sentimental. There is no proof of reincarnation. Even the clairvoyants who claim to have communed with the dead or disincarnate spirits have brought no proof to support their arguments. "We need something more than arbitrary theories about the 'immortal triad,' the 'three worlds,' the 'astral body,' the 'permanent atom,' or the 'Karma-Loka.' "[45]

Maeterlinck goes on to examine a host of related beliefs: telepathy, telergy, communication with the dead, and the findings related by the Society for Psychical Research. He quotes William James concerning hypnotism and the mediumistic seances James had attended. James believed that the series of coincidences he witnessed and those of which he had been informed confirm "the conviction that we are in the presence of an entirely new, improbable, but genuine phenomenon, which is difficult to classify among exclusively terrestrial phenomena."[46] There was a case, for example, in which a young girl, Josephine, had been hypnotized and regressed to an infantile state; then to former existences. When she regressed to an elderly man, her entire demeanor — voice, state of mind, conversation, description of life, relationships — changed. When incarnated into an old woman, she spoke in parched vocal sounds. Under hypnosis "a luminous aura" was observed around her, which became dark when Josephine was in between her two existences.[47]

Maeterlinck writes that James was fascinated with extraterrestrial phenomena: ESP, clairvoyance, telepathy. He was adamant about nothing, but investigated all. James did state, however, that he believed the body as well as moral and physical suffering disappear after death. Furthermore, man with his finite mind cannot understand the infinite (or expanded consciousness). There is an "antipathy" between consciousness and infinity. To use the word "consciousness" implies "a definite thing conceivable in the finite," whereas the infinite actually transcends comprehension.

Maeterlinck, like James, encourages inquiry into the mysteries of nature, the cosmos, and the human mind. He castigates the Christian church in its attempt at "narrowing" the "mystery of the universe"; on the contrary, man's vision must be broadened; the mind must be permitted to break out of the confines that enslave it and roam free. It must struggle heroically to experience the new, despite the fact that nature's secrets will never be revealed. "The unknown and the unknowable are necessary and will perhaps be necessary to our happiness."[48]

In order to motivate man — and himself accordingly — the search for the unknown must go on. To place restrictions on man's pursuits is to stunt him. These are the goals of all organized religious bodies, Maeterlinck claims. He felt no such barriers in his investigations. In his essay L'Hôte inconnu ("The Unknown Host," 1914), he inquired into premonitory dreams, telepathy, levitation, haunted houses, psychometrics, presentiments, and other inexplicable phenomena. These he evaluated in terms of their scientific validity and his own ideations.

The Unknown Host, which Maeterlinck defines as intuition, inhabits all beings. It is via this phenomenon that lucidity, clairvoyance, transmission of thought, and premonitory visions are possible. According to Dr. Osty, whom Maeterlinck quotes, "lucid subjects would act as mirrors in which latent intuitive thought in each one of us would be reflected . . . we ourselves would be lucid and they would merely reveal our own lucidity to us. Their mission would be to move, to awaken, to galvanize, to illuminate the secrets of our subconscious and compel them to rise to the surface of our normal life."[49] The intuitive faculty, latent in all people, would become, if properly trained or encouraged, a potent force. Once this inner energy is freed, communication with outside entities (beyond rational concepts of space and time) would become possible. Mediums in somnambulistic seances are examples of awakened or liberated intuitive faculties.[50]

Maeterlinck also believed in the cosmic implications of coincidences, in hypnosis and auto suggestion. Only by delving into the unknown without preconceived notions can one shed light on a tenebrous region within man's being, can one question the meaning of time and space. "What corresponds outside of ourselves to what we call time and space?" Maeterlinck mentions the "Apriorists," such as Kant, who believe that "the idea of time is innate . . . that time, like space, is an *a priori* form of our sensibility or an intuition preceding experience."[51] Maeterlinck concludes that such a concept does not really shed light on the notions of time and space; nor do the Empiricists, such as Marie-Jean Guyau, who believe that an "idea is acquired through experience" and that "time is the abstract formula for changes in the universe"; nor does Leibnitz's theory that space "is an order of coexistence and time an order of succession" go any further in enlightening mankind.[52] No one has been able to fathom the mystery of the universe. Man can merely posit, claim, inquire.

Maeterlinck believed that the dead are alive in another form within the universe. To communicate with such beings is possible through man's subconscious or his intuitive faculties. "Our subconscious must blend with everything that does not die in these beings, and that which does die in them is dispersed and loses all importance; it is nothing but the small consciousness which is accumulated on this earth and is maintained until the last hour by the fragile bonds of memory."[53] Whenever the "Unknown Host" manifests itself in man, it is an indication that "our I beyond the tomb," is already alive within us while we are still in bodily form. It unites what does not perish, momentarily, with those who have left their bodies." Since the "Unknown Host" lives within each of us and is immortal, it would follow that those who have died long ago are still alive, and that we may communicate with them at will. What Maeterlinck did not accept, however, was the limited form in which seances were handled and the materialistic aims for which they were given. He believed mediums and their adherents view intuitions into the past or future and communication with the dead as their own private domain to do with what they want, linked to their "insipid souvenirs" and their "mania for gossip."[54]

It is through the practice of psychometrics (clairvoyance, premonitory visions, transmission of thoughts, etc.) that one may communicate with the dead and not through what Maeterlinck labels as charlatanlike seances. Only when an individual has reached a higher state of consciousness, which enables him to make use of his intuitive faculties, can a rapport with another phase of existence come into being.[55] Maeterlinck quotes Dr. Geley who remarked that man's subconscious "is formed of superposed elements; it begins its journey from the unconscious world, which presides over the instinctive movement of the organic life of the species and the individual, then emerges via indiscernible gradations, until it rises to superior psychic life, the power and breadth of which seem to be unlimited."[56]

Maeterlinck was convinced that man could experience, but not understand, the mystery of the universe that enveloped him by delving "into one's depths, in the silence and night of our being, where agitation never ceases, and where destiny is formed." It is up to the individual to expand his consciousness by digging deep within himself, and in so doing uncover (discover) this hidden region. Each person must, therefore, practice the discipline of meditation if he is to unearth the secrets within his psyche.[57]

What did such an interest in psychic phenomenon indicate in terms of Maeterlinck and his time?

Maeterlinck's inner world seemed to be gaining more and more importance, whereas his existential world played a diminishing role in his life. This inward journey had always been characteristic of Maeterlinck, but more so since *The Blue Bird*. The afterlife in this play had been delineated in childlike terms. Yet, theosophical arguments and spatial and time concepts were implicit in the work.

Maeterlinck, nevertheless, was a product of his times. Prophetic dreams, coincidences, and mantic procedures had been studied since earliest times and had not always been relegated to the domain of superstition, ignorance, nonsense, or magic. Albertus Magnus, the great medieval magician, felt that coincidences and supernatural happenings which he described in his *Mirabilis Mundi* (1485), were an attempt by man to capture outer-worldly forces in order to understand and cope with them. The Bible, the Koran, the Book of the Dead, and the I Ching (considered as manifestations of divinity) also include atemporal happenings within their pages. Goethe, attempting to pin a scientific label on supernatural happenings, maintained in his *Conversations with Eckermann* that "We all have certain elective and magnetic powers within us and ourselves exercise an attractive and repelling force, according as we come in touch with something like or unlike."[58]

In the nineteenth century, there was increased interest in the psyche's participation in the universal mystery not only from poets and philosophers but from scientists and medical men as well. C. G. Carus, the Dresden-born physician to the king of Saxony, held that man's psyche was comparable to "a great, continuously circling river which is illuminated only in one small area by the light of the sun."[59] He divided the psyche into three distinct parts, each related to and working on the other. The conscious (or rational) function, which can comprehend the limited and temporal realm; the unconscious, which itself is divided into the relative (individual) unconscious and the absolute (collective) unconscious. The relative unconscious is that part of the unconscious which may become, or has been, conscious at one time, belonging to the individual (personal), and is subjectively experienced. The absolute (or collective) unconscious remains "inaccessible to the light of consciousness" except when it reveals itself in flashes of intuition, dreams, or in other ways, it is a limitless atemporal realm. As such, it is "a reservoir of our energies," and thus constitutes humanity's past that lives eternally within the individual and manifests itself in his present actions and thoughts, in this way playing a part in his future. "The key to an understanding of the nature of the conscious life of the soul lies in the sphere of the unconscious." Since the conscious is connected to the absolute or collective unconscious, each dependent upon the other, it affects the other in terms of the individual's actions, vis-à-vis himself and society at large. Carus wrote:

. . . we must realize that our unconscious life is affected by all humanity, by the life of the earth and by the universe, for it is definitely an integral part of this totality. The number of ways the unconscious is affected is infinite. The movement of the planets, other than the sun and the moon, affect our inner sentience, but to such a small degree that we may compare it to the earth's attraction to a falling stone . . . Changes in the atmosphere and in our planet's electric and magnetic currents, however, affect our unconscious life as deeply as do changes in the lives of human beings who are much closer to us. Indeed, the correlations in this sphere are most essential. At first, they are unconscious, although under certain conditions there may be communication from this dark realm to consciousness. Presentiments in dreams, empathy with events on the earth and in the heavens or in the fate of men, the astonishing magnetic rapport between distant persons, and other riddles whose solution normal psychology cannot provide may be fully explained only by these observations.[60]

The unconscious, then, is forever being tapped by the conscious and brought into cognition. Plato referred to the act of "cognition" as "remembrance" and defined it as "finding within," that is, going back to the absolute world of the unconscious.[61]

The discoveries of the following are all well known: Jean-Martin Charcot, at the Salpetrière Hospital in Paris, with regard to traumas in the symptomology of hysteria; Ambroise-Auguste Liébault and Hippolyte Bernheim, concerning hypnosis and auto-suggestion (*De la Suggestion dans l'état hypnotique*, 1884) in Nancy; Pierre Janet's inquiries into experimental psychology as expressed in his doctoral dissertation *L'Automatisme Psychologique* (1889); Freud's works, beginning with *Interpretation of Dreams* (1900); and Jung's *Psychology of the Unconscious* (1912).

That Maeterlinck should have been fascinated by psychic phenomena is understandable in view of the research being done in this field. What is of particular interest, however, is the fact that scientists were investigating a domain which had been heretofore relegated to the world of religion, mysticism, and superstition. The schism between the scientific world of positivism and the ambiguous, esoteric world of the mystic, which was predominant in the eighteenth century, had widened in the nineteenth, with Hippolyte Taine and Auguste Comte's scientific determinism. To restore some semblance of balance, a coalescing of opposites and a reshuffling of views was in order. A coming together of science and metaphysics occurred in the early 1900's and has continued to this very day. What had been strictly metaphysical has now become a source of study for the empirical physicist. Questions concerning ESP, premonitory dreams, and transmission of thought are not scoffed at any longer as superstitious nonsense; on the contrary, they are taken seriously by the scientist.

Maeterlinck posited the question of time and space and man's ability to transcend the differentiated world. What did such an idea imply in terms of the psyche? If precognitive dreams, prediction of events, ESP exist in the world of reality, does this mean that the psychic function exists outside of the "spatiotemporal law of causality?"[62]

Ever since Newton established his theory of causality man has been led to believe that everything within the universe has a causal explanation. If Newton's law was valid, then it might be postulated that chance itself would be the result of a causality which has not yet come into existence. But then how could one know about something which has not yet taken place? How could one explain telepathy or synchronicity?[63]

One must assume that causality is a philosophical principle that came into existence as a result of natural law. Modern physicists, whose conclusions are based upon spatial truths, consider the causal principle to be relative to some other factor (or factors) that is unfamiliar to man. An acausal event is virtually impossible to imagine. Since it is unthinkable to believe in anything which is not based on what we already know, we must conclude that acausal events appear in nature. Although the world of chance (or coincidences, precognitive dreams, telepathy) may seem frequently to be causally connected, in reality it is not. For example: if you buy a theater ticket with the same number as your house number printed on it, or telephone number, etc., or if you dream of

receiving a letter and it arrives the following day . . . .
Coincidences sometimes run in series: the cycles of a gambler, his
good and bad days. Einstein was impressed with Paul Kammerer's
experiments along these lines which had been written up in *Das
Gesetz der Serie*. Einstein did not relegate synchronistic events to
the realm of superstition or magic.[64]

Telepathy and precognitive dreams cannot be explained in terms
of the time and space factors since each breaches distance. The
psyche travels in a "variable space-time concept" or in another
dimension governed by laws and order that are foreign to us. One
may posit the belief that an acausal phenomenon (as in ESP) is an
energy relationship. But if the event has not yet occurred, how can
energy enter into the picture? Man's rational space-time concept is
an abstract intellectual notion, a hypothesis, as is his belief in
causality.[65] The psyche, on the other hand, functions in another
dimension and according to its own laws. Certain "patterns of
behavior" or archetypal patterns may be deduced from the psyche,
each giving off emotions or a "specific charge," but they cannot yet
be explained. When someone dreams or experiences certain
coincidences (synchronistic events), there are emotional aftermaths
to such occurrences. One is affected by certain "unconscious
instinctual impulses and contents." When the unconscious flows
into consciousness, it brings with it certain subliminal intuitions or
perceptions ("forgotten memory-images"). The images which
emerge may be acausal; that is, the individual experiencing them
cannot think of any connection between what happened in reality
and the occurrence in the dream. The images which have come into
consciousness, therefore, have no rational or causal relationship
with the objective situation the individual has just experienced — at
least, as far as he knows.

Some mantic processes, according to C. G. Jung, may be
explained in terms of emotions. By arousing someone's fears or
hopes (or interests), one stimulates some content within the
unconscious that then manifests itself in one or several archetypal
dream motifs. Such a situation might have been the case of poets
and their precognitive dreams or images. Many archetypal dreams
that are nourished in the collective unconscious include a collective
past and present, implying by the same token an abolition of what
rational man alludes to as time and space. Jung describes such

happenings in the following form:

The deeper "layers" of the psyche lose their individual uniqueness as they retreat farther and farther into darkness "lower down" that is to say, as they approach the autonomous functional systems, they become increasingly collective until they are universalized and extinguished in the body's materiality, i.e., in chemical substance. The body's carbon is simply carbon. Hence "at bottom" the psyche is simply "world."[66]

The "bottom" level to which Jung refers, lives within each being. It is a question of tapping such resources, lowering the threshold of consciousness (which comes automatically with *un abaissement du niveau mental*) that the individual experiences the effects which open the door to "absolute knowledge." As far as one knows, no mechanistic law exists that relates causal to acausal processes. Acausal phenomena is "the precondition of law, the chance substrata on which law is based."[67]

How else except by the acausal-factor theory, which permits the unconscious to exist and live beyond the physical space-time delineations, can one explain the vision of the eighteenth-century Illuminist, Jacques Cazotte, who foresaw his own death by the guillotine some thirty years before the event? who described in detail the death of Louis XVI, Condorcet, and others as they occurred and before they did?

The more scientists investigate the extratemporal, or what is alluded to today as the "subatomic" and the "supergalactic" spheres, the more aware they become of nature's diversity and man's longing to understand and regain a sense of his primordial unity — and the more "science parallels mysticism."[68]

Mystics such as Plotinus, Boehme, and Ruysbroeck believed in a world beyond the rational (or clock time), a world peopled with invisible entities. Philosophers and scientists have sought answers ever since the beginning of time. Democritus maintained that the universe is filled with atoms; Pythagoras, Plato, Nicolas de Cusa, Pico della Mirandola were convinced that the cosmos is a living entity. Kepler in his *Stella Nova* affirmed that one must go beyond the world of appearances to experience reality.

Nothing exists nor happens in the visible sky that is not sensed in some hidden manner by the faculties of Earth and Nature; (so that) these

faculties of the spirit here on earth are as much affected as the sky itself
. . . The natural soul of man is not larger in size than a single point, and on
this point the form and character of the entire sky is potentially engraved,
as if it were a hundred times larger.[69]

Leibnitz believed in the monad, the smallest entity of all.[70] As
science advanced, certain "elementary particles" (electrons,
protons, neutrons, etc.) [71] made up of matter were discovered to be
traveling through space, imposing their force in what looked like a
series of pathlike rows of tiny bubbles in a liquid. Because of the
energy aroused by these particles, physicists are able to examine
"the transformation of mass into energy and of energy into mass."[72]

More and more quantum physicists are drawn to a realm which
has heretofore only interested the mystic — that of acausal
phenomena. That such a working rapport may become even more
popular in the near future is not unthinkable. Let us recall that in
1956 the Atomic Energy Commission succeeded in isolating
neutrinos, "the most ghostlike of elementary particles." They were
alluded to as "ghostlike" because they have "no physical prop-
erties: no mass, no electric charge, and no magnetic field."[73]

Equally fascinating is Adrian Dobbs's theory that postulates "a
second-time dimension in which the objective probabilities of
future outcome are contained as compresent dispositional factors,
which incline or predispose the future to occur in certain specific
ways."[74] According to Dobbs's theory, a physical explanation for
telepathy, precognitive dreams, and hallucinations could be
forwarded. Dobbs employs the word "pre-cast" rather than "precognitive,"[75] indicating certain factors that could be perceived and
would predispose a happening "toward a given future state." But
such "pre-casts" are not merely haphazard, nor do they follow any
rational system that man knows of. The only way in which man can
discover anything about these factors is via a "hypothetical
messenger" which Dobbs labels "psitrons" and which function in a
second-time dimension. The psitrons are considered as having
"imaginary mass" (in the mathematical sense) and thus, according
to the theory of relativity, travel faster than light and definitely,
without loss of (imaginary) momentum.

Theories concerning "will influence" and "mind influence" were
posited by Sir John Eccles who believed that certain entities or

substances act upon neutrons in the brain and frequently influence brain activity in a startling manner.[76] Certain factors within the brain may increase or decrease its awareness, and expand its consciousness, thereby making telepathy, clairvoyance, and other acausal situations possible.[77]

The way in which energy is transformed into consciousness remains a mystery. That such questions have invaded the world of the scientist is particularly revealing. We may forward the belief that artists — in this case Maeterlinck — more sensitive than the average person, feel or intuit their way into other dimensions — magnetic fields that remain shut to the "normal" individual. Artists realized the validity of the acausal factor long before physicists began to concentrate their efforts on these matters.

IV   *World War I — The Activist*

The German invasion of Belgium in August 1914 brought Maeterlinck's metaphysical speculations to a halt. Fearing an immediate occupation of France, he and Georgette packed their belongings and left for "Les Abeilles" in Nice. As the war progressed and the Allies kept losing ground, political matters encroached upon his life. The suffering, the near-starvation diets, the atrocities inflicted on the Belgians, the deportation of countless citizens to German factories were more than he could bear; his detachment vanished. Emotions that had perhaps lain dormant within him for years suddenly became activated.

For the first time in his life perhaps, Maeterlinck sensed a feeling of solidarity with the Belgians. He was so strongly moved by these burgeoning emotions that he went to Rouen on August 2, 1914, and inquired as to whether he could join the French Foreign Legion, and the negative reply caused him much consternation. His age was the reason: he was then fifty-two years old. He could certainly be more helpful to the cause of the Allies with his writing than going into battle.

Maeterlinck took to his pen. His articles appeared in the London *Daily Mail*, the *Journal*, the *Figaro*, the *Petit Journal*. He traveled to Italy, England, and Spain where he delivered a series of pro-Ally speeches. Speaking before people or meeting strangers had always been anathema to Maeterlinck. For such a timid person to indulge in such work was indeed to show patriotism.[78]

Maeterlinck's political and socially oriented articles and speeches were written in what was for him a new style. Gone were the vaporous clouds, the phantasmagorias, the metaphysical presences, the *femmes fortes*. Maeterlinck dealt with life in a trenchantly realistic manner. He was intent on letting people know about his nation's plight and would spare no details. He praised the Belgians for their heroic soul and the extraordinary courage of their monarch, King Albert. Heretofore, Maeterlinck had considered the Belgian monarchy as conservative as its church, and only the socialist workers were to be praised. Now all divisiveness had vanished. The King as leader of a unified nation stood out as a solar force: "Of all the heroes of this enormous war who will survive in man's memory, one of the purest, one who inspires infinite love, will certainly be the young and great king of my small country."[79] Maeterlinck praised the soul of his people, their endurance, abnegation, and sacrifice. They were like the greats of old: Xenophon, Alexander the Great, William the Conqueror, Joan of Arc.[80]

Maeterlinck's admiration for the fortitude and integrity of the Allies was as unbounded as his hatred for the Germans, whom he called barbaric, ruthless, and heinous. He labeled their crime against humanity "inexpiable."[81] "I used to love Germany. I used to have friends there. Whether they are alive or dead now, they are in their tombs as far as I am concerned. I considered Germany great and honest . . . and it was always a friendly and well-wishing land. But there are crimes which annihilate the past and shut out the future. If I had not hated, I would have betrayed love." Maeterlinck had tried to separate the guilty from the innocent among the Germans, he had attempted to transcend petty national hatreds to reach the plateau of universal justice. But he could no longer overlook the ruins, the debris, the death he saw about him. His people were existing in a state of agony. The guilt for such massacres, Maeterlinck stated categorically, does not belong to the Prussians alone, but to the Germans as a whole. "It is untrue that out of this immense crime there should not be innocent and guilty ones, or degrees of guilt in such an onslaught; all those who have taken part are to be considered in the same category." All Germans were equally guilty: those who actively participated in the war, and those who failed to prevent it.[82]

Maeterlinck's trips to Rome, Milan, Florence, and Naples and the speeches he delivered in these cities were designed to win Italians over to the Allied cause. Until 1915 the Italians had professed neutrality, and Maeterlinck's words were designed to arouse them from their lethargy. "I do not have to recall the events which precipitated Belgium into an abyss of glorious pain . . . . This land has been punished as no other . . . for having done its duty . . . . It saved the world, knowing all the time that it could not be saved." Belgium, Maeterlinck pursued, is not only a land of heroes, but also one in which justice prevails.[83]

Maeterlinck's travels, speeches, and political tracts came to an end by 1917. Whatever reason motivated his return to "Les Abeilles", he remained there for the rest of the war. His own financial situation was rather shaky. The money he had placed in Belgian banks had diminished considerably and the funds accruing to him from Russia had been frozen.

At "Les Abeilles" he wrote a three-act drama, *Le Bourgemestre de Stilmonde* "The Burgomaster of Stilmonde," and a two-act sketch, *The Salt of Life*. In the foreward to the first play he called it "only a war and propaganda drama." He made no pretense to its qualities as a work of art. Shortly after its completion in 1917, it was translated into Spanish, English, and Swedish and produced in Buenos Aires in 1918, where it played for quite a while. Later it was performed in Spain, England, and the United States. The Anglo-American press labeled it "The Great War Play" and indeed it fulfilled that function. It aroused emotions and played on peoples' loves and hatreds. It was so moving that its production was banned in France. The government possibly feared that if French hatreds were aroused after the termination of the war, any kind of viable relationship with Germany would become an impossibility.[84]

The Burgomaster of Stilmonde takes place in a Flemish village that has been occupied by an Uhlan regiment. The Burgomaster's daughter, Bella, is married to Otto, a German, who is now a lieutenant in his country's army. The occupying German commander informs the Burgomaster that if any German soldier is hurt, the Burgomaster will be personally responsible and will have to pay with his life. When a Prussian officer is shot, Claus, a sixty-three-year-old villager whom the Burgomaster has known for years, is unjustly accused. The Burgomaster is executed. Bella is so horrified by her father's death and her husband's compliance with his commander's orders, she sends him away forever.

Although the theme of *The Burgomaster of Stilmonde* is far from new — marriage between people of enemy nations has happened from time immemorial — the characters are clearly delineated in true naturalistic style. The Burgomaster displays great courage at the right time, the daughter renounces her husband on philosophical issues and fatherly love, and the German acts in accordance with Prussian military discipline. Technically there is nothing new in Maeterlinck's play, but the development of the philosophical principles injects freshness into the drama. What is the value of a life? Is one life more important than another? Why should the Burgomaster save Claus's life, an old man who has lived a relatively mediocre existence, rather than his own, as mayor a person of importance in his village?

For the Burgomaster, life is of supreme importance regardless of class distinction. "The life of my old Claus is worth as much as my own, it is not a question of estimating the value or the usefulness of a life, but to find out whether or not I want to dishonor my own."[85] Bella is deeply pained by her father's decision. Yet she understands his reasoning. Otto cannot comprehend such "noble" sentiments. How could he, Maeterlinck reasons, since Otto belongs to a "barbaric race," a people devoid of feeling who terrorize nations, destroy, and mutilate.

Maeterlinck's passionate hatred for the Germans was so intense that no exceptions could be made. Germans were lumped together into a horrendous cesspool: "What can I say? One could not foretell that the Germans were going to massacre us and commit all the horror they are committing."[86] The Prussian commander is described as "hated by his men whom he treats like dogs."[87]

The Salt of Life takes place in a small frontier town between Holland and Belgium. Although it is labeled a "sketch" in Maeterlinck's foreword and is a thesis play, it is superior in structure and in character delineation to *The Burgomaster of Stilmonde*.

Dr. Floris Capelle has murdered a German officer who tried to rape his wife, Lena. He is imprisoned by the German occupation forces and is to be shot. His wife, who is much younger than he, adores him. She pleads his cause but is unsuccessful. When she hears of her mother-in-law's imminent death in another town across the frontier, she goes to the prison to speak to her husband and the

German commander. It is agreed that her husband will cross the border to see his mother, and she will remain as a hostage. The doctor departs. Hours pass. Finally he returns much to Lena's despair. She had hoped that her life would be taken rather than his. She begs to be shot instead of him. It is to no avail. Her husband's dying words to her: "Show people the nature of those who kill."[88]

Lena, the heroine, is a paragon of beauty and virtue. She is the self-sacrificing wife: gentle, subdued, and understanding. Unlike the dynamic and ultraheroic Monna Vanna and Mary Magdalene, or the determined Ariadne, or the fantasy figure Joyzelle, Lena breathes and lives courage because of the extreme integrity, balance, and harmony her love for her husband has inculcated in her. No longer modeled after the Georgette type of woman, Lena is the prototype of the charming Renée Dahon, Maeterlinck's bride-to-be.

It was perhaps Renée Dahon who inspired Maeterlinck to write a sequel to *The Blue Bird* entitled *Les Fiançailles* ("The Betrothal").

The play begins as a fairy visits Tyltyl who is now sixteen years old. She asks him if he has ever been in love. Embarrassed at such frankness, Tyltyl at first evades the question. The fairy prods him. He confesses that he has liked many girls: the woodcutter's daughter, the butcher's daughter, the maid at the inn, the beggar girl. The fairy commands that he must decide on one girl. She transports him into another domain. "You won't find them the same as they were in the other world," the fairy tells him, "because this is the real one and it's the truth in them that you will see here." The fairy describes the realm they visit as "purer and the light quite different . . . . We are now in a sphere in which men and women don't quarrel or wish one another harm."[90]

Tyltyl turns the sapphire stone given him by the fairy and the stage is flooded with a "supernatural light, investing all things with beauty, purity, and a transcendent joy."[91] He sees the girls he has known with new understanding and realizes, "When you love many, it merely shows that you haven't yet found the one whom you are to love."[92]

Tyltyl turns the sapphire stone given him by the fairy and the explains: "But I and the others are all you . . . ."[93] "Those who have lived in you live in you just as much as those who are going to. There is no difference; they all connect and it is still the same family."[94] Tyltyl meets his future children and they pick their mother-to-be. But Tyltyl does not yet recognize her. "Go away! You shan't have her until you know her!" the children cry out in annoyance. Tyltyl is stunned. "I believe they are right . . . . I believe it is really she."[95]

The vision is over. Tyltyl is at home again. His mother tells him of Mme Berlingot's impending visit with her daughter, Joy. When they arrive, Tyltyl is transfixed. It is the same girl he had seen moments before in another realm. "How long have you loved me?" he asks Joy. And she replies, ever since he gave her the Blue Bird as a child.[96] Nor had he forgotten her, he says. They both know at this instant that they will marry and have many children. Such is their destiny. It is their secret, however, until they grow up.

The Betrothal is as charming and delightful as *The Blue Bird*. It is Maeterlinck at his best: in the world of fantasy, naïve-childishness, where sentiments burgeon and the power of love is idealized. The play is also of philosophical import and designed to show man's oneness with nature as well as with past, present, and future. Such metaphysical notions have been described by Meister Eckhart as follows: "Here all blades of grass, wood, and stone, all things are One. When is a man in mere understanding? When he sees one thing separated from another. And when is he above mere understanding? When he sees all in all, then a man stands above mere understanding." When, for example, the fairy takes Tyltyl away from the mundane, phenomenological realm to the transcendental domain of cosmic consciousness, he can see into the very essence of matter. As Eckhart has stated: "The central silence is there where no creature may enter, nor any idea, and there the soul neither thinks nor acts, nor entertains any idea, either of itself or anything else."[97] When Tyltyl returns to his home he can distinguish form from essence. With his broadened vision, he knows his life's course and will proceed with resoluteness.

No matter how deeply Maeterlinck was drawn to mysticism, he could not be called a true mystic. A true mystic must pass through three phases of existence. First is the conscious existence, which permits an individual to relate to another in terms of the workaday world, second is the unconscious stage, which is experienced as a unifying agent, coalescing the disparate forces experienced by the creative artists in the form of thoughts, images, and sensations, and which emerge from the deepest strata of the psyche (the soul). The third phase belongs to the paradoxical domain of the mystic. It is here that oneness with the universe is known, where a *complexio oppositorum* occurs. Jakob Boehme experienced such a state in terms of the Godhead: "In this light my spirit saw through all things and into all creatures and I recognized God in grass and plants."[98] Such an egoless feeling is described in the *Upanishads*, the Near Eastern writings on the nature of man and the universe, which consider such a mystical experience as "going beyond the senses, beyond the understanding, beyond all expression . . . . It is the One without a second. It is the Self."[99] The Flemish mystic Ruysbroeck, whom Maeterlinck so admired, called the mystic "the God-seeing man" because "his spirit is undifferentiated and without distinction and, therefore, it feels nothing but the unity." Kant describes the experience of oneness as "the transcendental unity" of the self, a state "without any empirical content."[100]

Maeterlinck in his writings never reached the state of detachment, of oneness, known to the Buddhist, Christian, and Hebrew mystics, and which has been labeled as Nirvana, the Void, Emptiness, pure Nothingness, a desert, the wilderness, the Godhead. It is in such a state that all opposites vanish and paradoxes blend. Dionysius the Areopagite, wrote in these terms about God: "The dazzling obscurity which outshines all brilliance with the intensity of its darkness."[101]

Although well-versed in mystical literature and psychic phenomena, Maeterlinck never went beyond the stage of sensory-intellectual consciousness; the second step in the mystic's ascension, the area known to the creative artist who is forever tapping his collective unconscious. However, Maeterlinck's fascination with the domain of the mystic did not diminish; on the contrary, *Les Sentiers dans la montagne* ("The Paths in the Mountain") also written during the war, is made up of a collection of essays dealing with such hermetic subjects as: "The Power of the Dead," "Messages from the Other Side of the Tomb," "The Soul of Peoples," "Hope and Despair," "Macrocosm and Microcosm," "Heredity and Pre-Existence," "The Great Revelation," "Necessary Silence," "Karma."[102]

In the above-mentioned essays one comes away with the feeling that Maeterlinck is not yet definite as to what his credo is.

Certainly, he believes that the dead survive in each individual in the form of memories, and affirm their presence by arousing new ideas, stirring sensations, and thus bring about a new approach to life. "There are dead people whose élan surpasses death and finds life anew."[103] Maeterlinck was not in agreement with the contention of the English physicist and director of the Society for Psychical Research, who declared that "the dead do not die and can communicate" with the living.[104] Maeterlinck believed the English director was confusing the notion of death with "the intervention of unconscious intelligences" which permeate the atmosphere and which may affect individuals.[105]

For Maeterlinck, the dead live in the living in the form of character traits, physical characteristics, and ideations. He also maintains that personality or certain tendencies within the psyche are not inherited, but are experienced in image or sensation form and have been placed within the individual by those as yet unborn: "Heredity is an acquired fact, an experimental truth, pre-existence is a logical necessity."[106] What is to be born lives in germ form within each individual, if not materially then spiritually.[107]

In the fascinating essay "Two Lobes" Maeterlinck explains the differences existing between the Buddhist and Hindu concepts of reincarnation and the Occidental version of this belief. The Westerners believe reincarnation and its finale in Nirvana as being paradoxical in nature since it implies immortality and annihilation, flux and reflux, extroverted and introverted existence. According to the Hindu and Buddhist, however, Nirvana is an expression of "the great cosmic rhythm" that is basic to everyone's life and of which for the individual death is merely one of its "infinite pulsations."[108] For Maeterlinck, the Buddhist, and the Hindu no contradiction exists between the notion of reincarnation and Nirvana. Nirvana is not the annihilation of the individual, but rather his absorption into the All, the Totality. The Occidental, entrenched in the phenomenological world, can barely conceive of such a spiritualized concept. The Buddhist, who considers life and its many reincarnations as a series of sufferings, learns how to better himself in each succeeding incarnation, to become more detached from worldly matters: love, hope, desire, possessiveness and so on. When material and earthly necessities become meaningless to him, or when a "systematic and voluntary superdeath" takes possession of him (true death), Nirvana will be experienced. The Hinayana Buddhists describe Buddha's attainment — Nirvana — in the following manner.

Thereupon the Blessed One rising from the cessation of his
perception and sensation,
entered the realm of neither perception nor yet non-perception;
and rising from the realm of neither perception not yet non-perception,
he entered the realm of nothingness;
and rising from the realm of nothingness,
he entered the realm of the infinity of consciousness;
and rising from the realm of the infinity of consciousness;
he entered the realm of the infinity of space;
and rising from the realm of the infinity of space,
he entered the fourth trance;
and rising from the fourth trance;
he entered the second trance;
and rising from the second trance,
he entered the first trance;
and rising from the first trance,
he entered the second trance;
and rising from the second trance,
he entered the third trance;
and rising from the third trance,
he entered the fourth trance;
and rising from the fourth trance,
immediately The Blessed One passed into Nirvana.[109]

Nirvana may be looked upon as a psychic state that enables one to experience peace of mind, an end to sorrow, a termination in the series of reincarnations that is each person's *karma*. Maeterlinck defines karma as that "immortal entity which man forms by his acts and his thoughts and which follows or rather envelops and absorbs him throughout his successive lives and is modified as he is always modified, while at the same time conserving all anterior impressions."[110]

Although not yet convinced as to the validity of the concept of reincarnation as posited by the Buddhists, Maeterlinck did adhere to the notion of "continuous identity."[111] Such an ideation may be likened to the image of a wave floating on the ocean, or a collective rather than an individual identity. For example, is the wave we see

near the beach the same wave we saw further out in the ocean? The
Buddhist does not believe in "self-identical substance," but rather
in a "floating continuity." Maeterlinck accepted the notion of continuity in man's life, which could be compared to the stream of consciousness of his thoughts. Human beings remain the same, like
a wave rising and crashing down into the ocean. Many births and
deaths occur in a continuous motion in the time scheme of the past,
present, and future. The true mystic does not believe in the
phenomenological world of *Samsara*, that is, "the fleeting world of
temporal events," but rather in the continuous absorption in the
totality which is Nirvana.[112]

For Western mystics heaven means "the everlasting existence of
the individual human soul as an individual." For the Buddhist it
means that separate individuality ends but annihilation does not
take place. Most men, Maeterlinck believed, are unable to understand the abstract nature of most mystical concepts, and mankind as
a whole will never even come close to explaining the infinite
rationally. To reveal cosmic secrets to human beings may be
analogous to telling a dog how a clock works.[113] Certain secrets are
available to modern man; for example, the wisdom of the ancient
peoples who lived centuries back in Lemuria and in Atlantis. Their
secrets are buried in "the debris of esoteric traditions."[114]
Investigations into their past must be carried out: historical and
scientific inquiries into legends, myths, hieroglyphics, and the
strange monuments all over the world. There is also another method
we haven't yet approached scientifically: intuition. Such extreme
sensitivity will lead to deeper understanding of these last remaining
vestiges that are left to us.[115]

Maeterlinck quotes the writings of Roisel, whose volume on
Atlantis had impressed him: "It has been proven that long before
our historical times, the inhabitants of Atlantis had acquired
marvelous sciences, which humanity is just beginning to re-
constitute, whose haunting vestiges have been found among the
Gauls, Egyptians, Persians, Indians, and other ancient civilizations.
More than ten thousand years before our era, the Atlanteans were
familiar with the procession of the equinoxes, which are the silent
modifications that several constellations experience in their orbiting
the universe, and they also knew and used thousands of nature's
other secrets."[116]

Ancient continents and vanished civilizations have fascinated man ever since the dawn of history. Plato had mentioned Atlantis in *Timaeus;* the sacred texts of India had also alluded to similar continents and peoples. There exist occult fraternities which even today carry on the task of transmitting the secrets of humanity's knowledge to their initiates from one generation to the next.

New theories have burgeoned. Some scientists and archeologists now believe that interplanetary beings have visited earth some forty thousand years ago, and that the prehistoric airfield in the Andes Mountains is definite proof of their presence. It is claimed they not only taught mankind the arts but also produced the species *homo sapiens.*

Maeterlinck continually searched and inquired. It was the act of probing that absorbed him completely and permeated his psyche.

V   *Between The Two World Wars*

Maeterlinck married Renée Dahon on February 15, 1919.[117] They had planned to live quietly at "Les Abeilles" in Nice but were prevented from doing so by the honors that were bestowed upon Maeterlinck in what seemed to be an endless succession: in 1920 the Grand Cross in the Order of Leopold of Belgium; a doctorat *honoris causa* from the University of Glasgow.[118] Further excitement prevailed when Maeterlinck accepted an invitation to go to the United States. His admiration for the works of Emerson, Whitman, and Poe must have whetted Maeterlinck's appetite to see the new world.

Instead of finding a mystically and spiritually oriented land — a fitting backdrop to the notions he had nurtured of the United States — he was greeted by the "Blue Bird Campaign for Happiness." Stores with pictures and decorations of blue birds, banners with imprints of blue birds hanging across the streets, the crassest kind of advertising techniques possible emerged before Maeterlinck's eyes. Then came the interminable cocktail parties, celebrations, and fund-raising drives for various organizations.

The French were idolized in New York during this period. Other "greats" had displayed their talents in New York, which could boast of a large French colony. The inimitable French diseuse Yvette Guilbert sang her naughty songs and medieval ballads to enthusiastic audiences; Pierre Monteux, the conductor; Jacques

Thibaud, the violinist; Robert Casadessus, the pianist; the Capet quartet; Jacques Copeau, the founder of the Vieux-Colombier theater in Paris and his troupe had all visited New York. Now, it was Maeterlinck's turn to astound Americans.

He was obliged to attend certain functions and to give a series of lectures. He had to be present at the musical version of *The Blue Bird* and at Debussy's opera *Pelléas and Mélisande.* Maeterlinck, who was nearly tone deaf, was sure that Debussy's opera would be an ordeal for him. When in 1902 Debussy refused to let Georgette Leblanc sing role of Mélisande because he found her voice wanting and asked instead the unknown Mary Garden to create the role, Maeterlinck declined to attend a performance. Now on December 27, 1920, he finally heard the music, and he was so deeply impressed by the timber and quality of Miss Garden's voice and the depth of her portrayal that he wrote her a note: "For the first time I have entirely understood my own play, and because of you."[119]

Sam Goldwyn invited Maeterlinck to California presumably to write film scenarios. Although he wrote three of them, only two scenarios are extant, *The Blue Feathers* and *The Power of the Dead.* Goldwyn used none of them. Maeterlinck lectured in San Francisco, Los Angeles, and Berkeley but did not feel at home in the casual atmosphere of California. He needed solitude and privacy. Neither was possible in the West. Moreover, Maeterlinck took umbrage at the openness and what he claimed to be the Americans' lack of etiquette and refinement.

The Maeterlincks returned to Nice in May, 1920, and remained there until 1939. Their life of seclusion was broken every now and then with short trips to Spain, Belgium, Paris, and Portugal.[120]

Still interested in the theater, Maeterlinck decided to try his hand at yet another drama: *La Puissance des morts* ("The Power of the Dead"). He did not realize that he had not grown with the times. The well-made play so popular at the turn of the century, as exemplified by Brieux, Bernstein, and Curel, was now rejected. New directors, trained by Jacques Copeau at the Vieux-Colombier (Louis Jouvet and Charles Dullin) and others (Jacques Pitoëf and Gaston Baty) were setting out on their own rigorous road. They sought to achieve harmony in producing methods: that is, they believed that the dramatist, the actor, and the audience must be linked in a bond of mutual effort, understanding, and participation. Some of the young directors even claimed that when unity among actors, authors, and audience was achieved, a mystical force penetrated the actor and endowed him with hypnotic power, bringing his acting to a fine edge. The directors were certain that when this potent force took hold, the play moved on as if by itself, unfolding almost miraculously. There was no sense of strain, rather, a refreshing sense of release and exaltation that permeated the performers and the audience. Both spectators and actors had been sensitized by the medium, the play, from which a world of fancy had arisen of unusual breadth, drive, and vitality. A dramatic work, an evening's entertainment should be a conversation, the young directors believed, between author, actor, and audience.

Maeterlinck was still writing melodramas, thesis plays — and now a thriller. *The Power of the Dead* has none of the fresh vigor or originality of his first plays, nor the verve and poetry of the new dramas being shown in the France of the early 1920's. Yet it does have suspense.

The Power of the Dead, a four-act drama, takes place in Flemish Flanders in a Gothic castle, eerie in its decay. Jean d'Ypermonde, having gambled his money away, returns to his castle. He confides to Pierre, the brother of his fiancée, Jalline, that he is unworthy of her, that he is heavily in debt. Pierre counters by telling him that Jalline loves him, that "she is one of those women that only love once in their lives." Unknown to the audience, the following scenes (the bulk of the drama) takes place in Jean's dream world, not in the existential domain. Jean dreams he has killed the man who had lent him the money he used for gambling; that he is tried but because of circumstantial evidence Pierre is accused of the crime instead and goes to prison. When Jean awakens, Jalline is there and embraces him. He realizes all had been a dream. Yet this dream is considered as intervention from his unconscious (or from another world). The dream has made him aware of all that he had at stake. "I have seen all that I was on the point of losing," he tells Jalline. "And I see all that I have found again!"[121] Jean is convinced that his father (who also played a part in the dream) as well as his ancestors, had protected him. "They are in my heart of hearts, in my blood, in my soul, and in my whole real life. They live as much as ourselves, since they are alive in us as we are alive in and through them!"[122]

The Power of the Dead expresses the spiritual turmoil of a man at the crossroads: a being so troubled by material problems that his anguish overcomes his faculty to reason. Jean anticipates the worst. He could, therefore, explore his anguish only through the dream, his irrational domain. His rational function had come to a standstill, lacking both focus and direction. It was only through the unconscious, which he understood as a phenomenon peopled with his ancestors, that he learned to cope with his existential plight.

The Power of the Dead is a blend of Ibsen and Strindberg with a bit of gruesome terror à la Poe. The blend of ultrarealism and supernatural phenomena makes for potent excitement during the reading of the play. Yet poetry and lyricism are wanting, and the characters are banal. No lasting impression remains with the reader.

The supernatural, the occult, and the religious bent clearly delineated by Maeterlinck in *The Power of the Dead* was to be further investigated in his next volume, *Le Grand Secret* ("The Great Secret," 1921).

In *The Great Secret*, a vast study of occultism, he discusses the Vedic teachings, those of Osiris and Zoroaster, the astrological speculations of the Chaldeans, the pre-Socratic philosophers of Greece, the Neoplatonists, the Kabbalists, the Hermetists of the Middle Ages, and the nineteenth-century theosophists. After this historical investigation Maeterlinck concludes that God is unknowable. As always, he rejects revelation and revealed religions — the four great ones: Hebrew, Christian, Mohammedanism, Buddhism. Yet Maeterlinck is fully aware of man's need for religion; it is a useful weapon to keep the masses in check. God exists everywhere and is in man, inside and outside of him. At death, man's divine part continues to exist not as an individual self but as part of a collective totality.

From 1921 to 1923 Maeterlinck published virtually nothing. He did write a one-act "bedroom farce," *Berniquel*, which Lugńe-Poë produced and which starred Mme Maeterlinck. Although a humorous satire on adultery, it was not of import. Maeterlinck spent most of his time at Nice. Every now and then he went to Royat for the waters. The doctors had told him he had a minor heart problem. His life of *dolce far niente* continued.

Although Maeterlinck's religious ideations did not alter considerably throughout the years — he had been a confirmed agnostic ever since he left the College of Sainte-Barbe — his political views had changed considerably. Before and during World War I, he had been a socialist. By 1923 he was an ultrarightist. He supported the Action Française but not all of their politics, which included the restoration of monarchy, an alliance between Roman Catholicism and the state, and an anti-Semitic campaign. He did wish to see a stronger and more unified rule. During a trip to Italy in 1923, Maeterlinck approved and found appropriate Mussolini's conquest of Abyssinia: "This essentially primitive nation really needed to be regenerated for an exploitation profitable to all civilized peoples."[123]

Maeterlinck's literary taste was ebbing as rapidly as his political acumen. Marcel Proust, whose death in 1922 had caused a void in the literary world, was derogated by Maeterlinck. He labeled Proust's supporters, the members of the *Nouvelle Revue Française*, "snobs." One may perhaps attribute Maeterlinck's distaste for Proust and for the members of one of the finest literary magazines of the period, staffed by such writers as Gide, Copeau, Ghéon, Rivière and others, as an indication of his own inability to evolve as a writer. Maeterlinck's talents as a dramatist seemed to have gone dry. He could no longer find a common denominator between himself and the emerging literary groups: Giraudoux, Claudel, Lenormand, Valéry, Breton — men who were to impress their names on the literary world.

Trips to the Near East and to North Africa enlivened Maeterlinck's calm existence. One tragic event impinged upon what could have been a great joy in his life: on May 12, 1925, Mme Maeterlinck gave birth to a stillborn child.

Maeterlinck's meditations continued — always delving into the enigma of the cosmos: first as an entomologist, then in scientific terms discussing the laws of attraction and dimension.

Maeterlinck's first series of volumes dealing with entomology included *La Vie des termites* ("The Life of the Termite," 1927), *La Vie des fourmis* ("The Life of the Ant," 1930), and *L'Araignée de verre* ("The Glass Spider," 1923). He studied the insects in question and their environment with expertise and considered them as an example of God's inability to create a perfect form. God's supreme failure, of course, was his creation of man, whose weaknesses become more and more apparent with the passing of years.

The most interesting of the three volumes in Maeterlinck's entomological series is *The Life of the Termite*. It is a pessimistic work in which Maeterlinck compares man's future existence with that of the termite who inhabits a world of darkness, feeds on its own dejecta and dead, and lives in a collective and utilitarian society. "Is what the termites present to us a model of social organisation, a picture of the future, a sort of 'anticipation' "? Is this the goal to which we ourselves are tending?"[124]

Maeterlinck is highly impressed with the termites' extraordinarily well-organized society. They are remarkable technicians, he asserts, in that they construct intricate galleries beneath the surface of the earth out of the debris of wood which they have kneaded and mixed with fecal matter. [125] Their society is communistic and matriarchal. All labor for the benefit of the queen. Based on a division of labor, each termite has his function: workers, soldiers. The soldiers are like a group "of monsters escaped from a nightmare," writes Maeterlinck.[126] They are reminiscent of the most fantastic and horrendous visions of a Bosch, Breughel, or Callot. Their heads are phenomenally large for their bodies; their mandibles are voluminous. The entire insect looks like a giant horn shield bearing a pair of scissorlike pincers similar to those of a lobster. The queen's sole function is to lay eggs. She is nothing but a "gigantic swollen stomach." As for the king, he lies under the queen and must fertilize her. Hundreds of workers stand in front of the queen's mouth and feed her the privileged food, while at the other orifice, another crowd of termites gathers the eggs as they drop from her. Soldiers are all about. They keep the circulation of termites going in orderly fashion. As soon as the queen proves to be barren, she is left to die. This is accomplished by stopping her food intake. After her demise, she is devoured. Nothing is wasted in this utilitarian society.

The utopists, Maeterlinck suggests, who search out the most incredible types of governments for some future ideal society, have merely to look beneath their feet — at the termites' fantastic way of life. It may be premonitory on Maeterlinck's part, but he feels that if society continues to develop along the same lines it has in the past, man may find himself experiencing an existence reminiscent of that of the termite.[127]

Certainly Maeterlinck's vision of man's future was far from

reassuring. To live in such a well-organized society is to divest it of any imaginative or creative faculties. That would be anathema for him or anyone interested in the arts. Turning his attention toward outer space, toward the world of the physicist, the mathematician, and the astronomer, Maeterlinck completed three more long works: *La Vie de l'espace* ("Life of Space," 1928), *La Grande Féerie* ("The Great Fairyland," 1929), and *La Grande Loi* ("The Great Law," 1933).

In the first volume of this trilogy, Maeterlinck inquires into the "enigma of dimensions." In the second volume, *The Great Fairyland*, he explicates the latest development in cosmic inquiry with regard to astronomy then philosophizes about divinity. One must not, he asserts, ask the question as to whether the universe is evolving, where it is going. To posit such queries is, in Maeterlinck's words, puerile. "The universe, in fact, can go nowhere since it is everywhere. It can attain nothing since there is nothing outside of itself. Filling everything, it is immobilized by itself, for all time; it is fixed in space-time or, rather, in infinity-eternity. The universe, which we would do well to call God if this word did not instantly awaken overly anthropomorphic and excessively naïve images, can neither evolve materially nor spiritually, nor go from worse to better. If it did, it would imply another universe with a superior God who would see to such evolution; then this other universe or this superior God would be the real God or the veritable universe capable of budging and finding itself (Himself) in turn prisoner of its (His) own infinity."[128] The universe, for Maeterlinck, is immobile, immutable, and imperfectible. The same does not hold true for its adjuncts or parts. Everything within the universe — from the smallest particle to the largest entity — is in a perpetual state of flux and can, therefore, perpetually change form in an ascending or descending order.[129]

Divinity may never be defined, Maeterlinck states, though scientists have made strides in their attempts to explain the time and space factors he associates with God. "God is the universe which is before anything else infinite space and time in its unlimited form: eternity."[130] The Greeks, Maeterlinck points out, had also associated God with the time-space factor. Cronos, the father of Zeus, who was the creator of the world, was confused in later times with Chronos, the god of time, the supreme divinity above which only destiny reigned. Destiny in turn is nothing but the "unfolding of time on earth, that is to say, our space-time concept in another form."[131]

The philosopher-mathematician Alfred North Whitehead also attempted to define God in *Science and the Modern World*. His conclusions are no more specific than those of the mystics living centuries back. Whitehead did not believe in a perfect or omnipotent God, but rather in the notion of a God who is interdependent with the world and developed with it. He declared that God was an entity which lives "beyond, behind, and within the ephemeral flux of immediate things," a force which is real and yet is to be realized, a far-reaching possibility and a present reality, that which gives meaning to everything and eludes apprehension, a goal that is beyond the reach of everything, something which is supreme, the ideal, and yet a hopeless quest.[132]

There was no question in Maeterlinck's mind that mathematicians and mystics were meeting on equal ground at this time in man's development; just as the mathematicians had perceived a four-dimensional figure through their inner eye, so the mystics (from Pythagoras to Plato, to Boehme) experienced God in a similar inner vision.

In *The Great Law* Maeterlinck opts for Newton's law of gravity because the cosmos remains infinite and not as Einstein's followers would have it, finite but without limits. "Newtonian physics and mechanics admit that they know nothing as to what gravitational force is in itself, and how it can operate instantaneously across the most fantastic distances. They simply study its effects and relegate the rest to the rank of unfathomable mysteries, such as life, being, infinity, eternity, time, space, and, in general, if you look into the depths of things, nearly all that exists." And Maeterlinck pursues, "The Einsteinians, on the other hand, do not own up to anything and claim that the notion of force is a creation of our minds which corresponds to no reality in nature where there are no forces but deformations and movements. It is the acceleration of these movements which causes the phenomena of gravitation."[133]

It is interesting to note that Maeterlinck, a playwright, philosopher, botanist, entomologist, expanded his intellectual realm to include mathematics and physics. That he should have attempted to discuss the complex notions of Einstein or Newton in such chapters as "Universal Gravitation and Centripetal Force," "Universal Rotation and Centrifugal Force," and "The Expansion of the Universe," when he was not trained in higher mathematics or physics, is rather presumptuous. This entire series, though interesting from a philosophical point of view — and surely an example of what psychologists term inflation — is riddled with subjective and unscientific statements. The only valid point Maeterlinck makes is that no matter how man has tried to solve the mysteries of God and the cosmos, he flounders in a sea of enigmas. Maeterlinck further intimates that man, and particularly the scientist, should be more humble. The same might be said of Maeterlinck himself.

In his following six volumes, which the French critic Henri Bidou labeled "the Pascalian series," Maeterlinck inquires still further into the nature of God, Is there a God? What is the meaning of religion, its function? Are churches a valid way of worshiping divinity? What place does the mystic occupy in modern society? Is evil a viable force? Does man possess free will? Is he isolated on this planet? Is the moral nature of man base and corrupt as the Scriptures claim? Has man progressed? In *Avant le Grand Silence* ("Before the Great Silence," 1934), *Le Sablier* ("The Hourglass," 1935), *L'Ombre des ailes* ("The Shadow of Wings," 1936), *Devant Dieu* ("Before God," 1937), *La Grande Porte* ("The Great Door, 1938), *L'Autre Monde ou le Cadran stellaire* ("The Great Beyond," 1942) Maeterlinck sums up his credo.

He opposed organized and revealed religions as well as the notion of hell and sin; nor did he believe in a personal, creative deity. He was certain that no one will ever know whether there is a God or whether a future life awaits man. The need for religion, he asserts, is based on fear and anguish with regard to damnation, everlasting punishment, and torment. Maeterlinck defines his God as a transcendental phenomenon. "He is the flower of our soul, the summit of our I, more I than the rest of our Us. He is our incessant creation. He changes from century to century, from age to age, day to day."[134] Humanity must enlarge its view of divinity and associate it with time, which is immobile: "He is immobile as space and eternity are. He is space and eternity."[135]

Maeterlinck's view of God had changed considerably from his early days. When he wrote *Pelléas and Mélisande*, he let the senex figure declare: "If I were God, I would have pity in my heart for men." Now Arkel would say: "If I were God, I would be ashamed of having created mankind."[136]

If God was the Creator, if He sent his son Christ to redeem mankind from its sins, it was He who implanted these sins into mankind. Why did He fashion an imperfect being such as man? What was the point of Creation? To limit the notion of God, to try to answer man's persistent questions about the ways of divinity, to attempt to rationalize cosmic ways and set them into a mold, as is the case with all organized religions, is to belittle what is immutable, eternal, and infinite.

In *The Hourglass* Maeterlinck admits his ignorance and inability to pursue the question of divinity any further. "I confess at the very beginning that I know nothing. Let him who believes that he knows the truth tell me what it is; I should accept it with gratitude if it seemed acceptable. I, hitherto, have not discovered it; which is why I am still looking for it, on my right hand and on my left, before me and behind, in the light and in the shadows . . . . I say honestly what I observe, without adopting any definite point of view, although I should be very glad to possess a definite standpoint."[137]

Maeterlinck further suggests that man, particularly with regard to industrial nations, should work in harmony with nature. Nature has given him his intelligence, his reason, his weapons. Nature is man's inspiration. If he attacks this universal and eternal force, if he belittles it, he will harm himself and divest himself of his sustenance both spiritually and physically.[138] Man should humble himself before this mysterious realm and should replenish the earth each time he divests it of some part of its power. Maeterlinck warns future civilizations of nature's capacity for revenge — the ability to grow barren, to send tidal waves, floods, droughts — in an attempt to set man back in his place.

Even in death, nature is a source of comfort and strength. Although man loses his "intellectual consciousness," he retains his "true consciousness, which has no temporal or personal memories but the eternal and universal memories of the race, of the species, of the electrons."[139] Because man is endowed with both a personal and impersonal faculty, he may be able to communicate with his ancestors since they are alive in everyone in the form of "invisible cells"; each being may therefore profit from the experiences of past generations. It is through the past (through chromosomes and hormones, which live on from generation to generation) that wisdom is acquired. Many people are unaware that such communication between past and present is actually occurring in the "subconscious or the supraconscious sphere."[140] The power of communication between present and past exists in the innermost parts in man, Maeterlinck concludes, and "we have not yet succeeded in raising these communications to the level of the will and understanding."[141] If man's will and his thinking principle can seize these messages his deepest unconscious holds, then he will make enormous strides, benefiting from "eternal time" — the mystic's cyclical space-time credo. Memory will be so refined as to make the deepest perceptions possible regardless of the impediments the rational mind places in its path. Maeterlinck and Bergson share the same opinion with regard to memory: "Memory is the point of intersection between spirit and matter," writes Bergson.[142] But Maeterlinck goes on to say that such a statement is actually devoid of meaning, "for spirit and matter being but one, they have no point of intersection. Spirit is matter that remembers; and matter is spirit that forgets."[143]

In *The Shadow of Wings, Before God, The Great Door,* and *The Great Beyond* Maeterlinck pursues his philosophical, scientific, and metaphysical investigations. His pessimism is trenchant in these books. Man has not progressed, he asserts, and he is still at the same point "when attempting to define the workings of the soul and mind, the reason for earthly suffering," the knowledge concerning identity, past, present, "and so many terrifying questions that we have addressed for centuries to the ever silent heavens."[144]

Man is predestined. He is not master of his will. When evil or pain encroaches upon him, man finds himself weakened by anguish and no longer able to fight back to transcend the wretchedness of his human condition. At the height of his career, Maeterlinck had believed that wisdom, instruction of the deepest kind, could elevate man and help him overcome his miseries. Now Maeterlinck had regressed to his earlier position outlined in *The Intruder* and *The Death of Tintagiles.* All is preordained, perhaps even before birth. It is almost as if Maeterlinck had combined the powerful Greek concept of destiny and the Jansenist edict of predestination with the scientific laws of heredity. The chance factor intruded only in a limited way, and when it did, its results were most frequently negative.

Maeterlinck had stepped away from the Stoicism preached by Seneca and Marcus Aurelius to which he had adhered. He no longer felt the mind could control the body, that man's will would compel him to act in an ascending order. The notion of happiness or joy is an illusion, a fallacy. It is based on memory that is not an exact replica of past events but one that alters with changing moods. Memory distorts "reality" and consoles, and if need be, permits individuals to escape from the pains of present existence.

Maeterlinck's God "is the God who does not yet exist. As soon as I shall believe I know Him," he writes, "I shall not believe in Him any more."[145] To reject the notion of God would be to disbelieve in oneself, since both man and divinity are inextricably linked. Since man and God are synonymous, Maeterlinck continues, "To cease searching for God means to lose Him and to lose oneself without any hope."[146]

Although Maeterlinck's philosophical inquiries are far from original, they are unique in that they sum up the hopelessness and the pessimism of a whole prewar generation. The march of science, industry, and technology had done little to avert the evils of possessiveness, aggression, and destruction. Maeterlinck was fully aware of this solemn moment in history: the war clouds that were gathering, quickly and mercilessly, from the north. Organized religions as a whole had done little to elevate man's morality! God's emissaries to this earth still less!

VI *The Exile*

Maeterlinck had been an outspoken foe of the Germans during World War I. His only comfort at the time had been the pride he took in the heroism of his people and their monarch, King Albert of Belgium. The situation at the outset of World War II had altered drastically. King Leopold III, Maeterlinck alleged, was a traitor to his people and a disgrace to his country.

As the German invasion proceeded and country after country was invaded and people tortured and scattered, Maeterlinck grew disconsolate. At seventy-seven years of age, he wondered where he would go if France were to be occupied. He was sure he would be shot or imprisoned for the anti-German statements he had made throughout the years. He thought of seeking refuge in Spain, but that was not feasible; Generalissimo Franco had shown himself sympathetic to Hitler. Portugal remained a possibility, all the more inviting since Maeterlinck had become quite friendly with that country's dictator, Dr. Antonio Salazar.

Maeterlinck admired Salazar as a friend and as a political leader. When in 1928 Salazar had been given financial control of Portugal, he had succeeded, for the first time in the twentieth century, in creating a financially stable economy. Four years later he was made premier and dictator of a land where the church reigned virtually supreme. The Constitution of 1933 enabled Salazar to establish a corporative state with a regimented economy. With the end of popular elections, peace and stability were a certainty.

The Maeterlincks went to Lisbon in 1939 where in November he was awarded the Order of St. James of the Sword. The Theatro Nacional in Lisbon presented Maeterlinck's new play *L'Abbé Sétubal* ("Father Setubal") in April 1940. Salazar and high officials of the Roman Catholic Church attended the première.[147]

Father Sétubal is a mediocre play. It is interesting only as an expression of Maeterlinck's views with regard to Roman Catholicism and its doctrine of sin, confession, and absolution. Heretofore Maeterlinck had been anticlerical, castigating the church when he felt it necessary and denigrating many of its official doctrines. Indeed, he completely rejected organized religions. His essay *Death* had been considered heretical by the Roman Catholic Church and had been placed on the Index in 1914. Strangely enough, in *Father Sétubal* the church and its doctrines are lauded; its authority is supreme. Two reasons may account for such an about-face. Maeterlinck considered the church a necessary evil because it kept the masses in check making them fearful, thus obedient, and giving them solace, therefore comfort. Secondly, he might have felt such a gesture to be politically expedient having been invited to remain in Portugal at a critical time in history.[148]

Father Sétubal opens as the venerated abbess of Fontmagne confesses to having poisoned Father Macial, whom she believed to be a threat to the church's power. Before her death she requests absolution from Father Sétubal. He refuses to pardon her unless she admits her crime openly. To accede to such a demand would be to create a scandal within the church. The abbess dies. The pharmacist

accused of murdering Father Macial awaits execution in prison and
Father Sétubal is torn by conflict. He cannot let an innocent man
die for a crime he has not committed, nor can the priest violate the
secret of confession. He decides to confess to the crime himself.
After all, he reasons, Christ died for mankind; so he, a priest, will
expiate a crime by sacrificing himself. In a drawn-out court scene in
which the beauty of sacrifice is lauded, a *deus ex machina* ending
exonerates Father Sétubal and the innocent man.

The most surprising feature of Maeterlinck's play emerges from
the puerility of the arguments involved. When writing such
fantasies as *The Blue Bird*, *The Betrothal*, and *Pelléas and
Mélisande*, the beauty, imagination, lyricism, and fairy tale quality
captivated audiences. In *Father Sétubal* spectators are confronted
with a series of infantile arguments rendering the church and
divinity uninteresting and ridiculous.

Even more distasteful is the rejection of truth as dramatized in
Father Sétubal and as seemingly implicit in church doctrine. The
fact that the abbess murdered a man is of little import. What counts
is the fact that scandal must be avoided at any cost, even at the
price of integrity. The goal of the abbess, the priest, and the bishop
was to hide the crime, thus obliterating truth. Was Maeterlinck
implying that the church was so weak an institution as to be unable
to afford a scandal? that it was tottering on the brink of collapse?
Would it not have been more heroic — though dangerous — to
bring the crime out into the open, rather than resorting to devious
methods to keep such evil hidden? One comes away with the
feeling that Maeterlinck looked at the church as a perfect vehicle to
keep a populace in ignorance, like little sheep or children who must
be presented with a perfect institution so that faith in its infallibility
will never waver.

As the war raged, Maeterlinck feared that even Portugal might
fall to the Nazis. He looked toward the United States as a land of
refuge. Well-known artists and writers had and would come to this
shore in search of asylum: André Maurois, Henri Bernstein, Jules
Romains, Marc Chagall . . . .

Maeterlinck, his wife, her parents, two dogs, and two birds left
for New York on July 12, 1940. When settled in the United States
Maeterlinck planned on pursuing his career as a dramatist. The reply was negative when he attempted to have his play *Jeanne d'Arc*

("Joan of Arc") produced. Although the subject was appropriate in 1940 — the times were harrowing and a heroine of such caliber would have been a morale-raiser — Maeterlinck unfortunately did not dramatize Joan of Arc's military victories nor her vision, but rather her trial and burning at the stake. Neither was *Father Sétubal* produced in New York. Rather than face the fact that the play was unappealing, the Maeterlincks put the blame elsewhere. "There was no chance," said Mme Maeterlinck, "of getting it produced in New York because the Protestant Americans are ignorant of what the secret of the confessional is and cannot be interested in it."[149] To castigate others for one's own failings is indeed the simplest escape route. Maeterlinck felt no need to come to grips with the painful realization that his imagination had withered. Yet, he persisted. He wrote *Les Trois Justiciers* ("The Three Justiciaries," probably written in 1942), *Le Jugement dernier* ("The Last Judgment," probably written in 1944), *Le Miracle des mères* ("The Miracle of the Mothers," unpublished), and a sketch *L'Enfant qui ne veut pas naître* ("The Child Who Does Not Want to Be Born," 1942).[150]

The Three Justiciaries may be thought of as a liturgical drama, more palatable than *Father Sétubal*. Audiences are introduced to a greedy, lustful egocentric Solomon who seeks to diverst his ward, Tristanelle, of her inheritance. The Rebellious Shadow (Solomon's conscience) makes him increasingly aware of his negative ways. The conflict between Solomon's conscience and his desires comes to a climax one day as he stands by a river and sees a woman screaming hysterically — her little boy has fallen into the water and is being carried away by the current. Although he cannot swim, Solomon jumps into the water and saves the boy "miraculously." An unhappy individual prior to this act, Solomon is now at peace with the world. He restores Tristanelle's inheritance to her and looks forward to happy days ahead.

In *The Last Judgment* Maeterlinck treats the theme of death. The play opens in a cemetery. Adults, children, priests, many people arise from their graves and begin the routine of life once again. They are unaware of the fact that they are dead. They meet three archangels: Gabriel, Raphael, and Michael, all of "miraculous beauty" and clothed in "floating garments," reminiscent of the angels depicted by Botticelli and Mantegna. The archangels inform the group that there is no hell and there are no demons. The bishop who has been shuddering with fear until now replies with pleasure: "I no longer have anything to ask of God." But then he asks: Who tempted Jesus? Who pursued him? "Evil thoughts of man" that had to be concretized, "rendered visible" is the reply, otherwise man would not have taken them seriously and would not have tried to redeem himself. The people are then informed that the dead are resurrected if they are good. They must review their lives: they must die in order to be reborn. In Act II the resurrected are in heaven. Gabriel tells them that the God they had envisaged — with white beard and sitting on a throne, and the son of God in porcelain as depicted in pious images in cathedrals and churches — are false views. When you look at God, Gabriel asserts, "you will see nothing since he is everywhere, you will have to learn to discover him in space and in time, he will appear to you in the form you deserve and you will begin searching for him until he resembles his essence in you."

Not only is *The Last Judgment* poorly constructed, the contradictions and naïvetés are also surprising. Although he asserts the fact that God is amorphous, Maeterlinck nonetheless takes great pains in the drama to materialize all aspects of the heavenly sphere: beautiful angels, superb virgins, harps, clouds, and pastel colors. Where then is the totally spiritual and nonanthropomorphic concept of God? Even more unpalatable is that some of the dead — Judas, Torquemada, Hitler — will not be resurrected; whereas those who have died in battle in defense of their country will rise instantly to the heavenly throne. "Their souls are already at the feet of the Almighty. They neither have to transfigure their memories nor purify their bodies in divine blood, they earned the right to eternal life at their death." It is understandable that Maeterlinck as a humanitarian would have implanted this comforting thought into his play when so many young men were dying at the front. As an artist and philosopher, however, it contradicts his previous arguments that God is infinite, omnipotent, omniscient and must be conceived in terms of the space-time concept; that the notion of sin, absolution, damnation — all features of organized religions — are false.

During his stay in the United States Maeterlinck busied himself writing plays, articles, a ballet *(The Dance of the Stars)*; he also lectured. His volume of Memoirs, *Bulles Bleues* ("Blue Bubbles") is delightful. A "happy" work, he wrote in his preface, filled with joyful reminiscences — a segment of his youth, his hopes and ideals.

The years passed slowly despite the fact that he was active lecturing and attending receptions, cocktail parties for French War Relief, and other charitable functions. He also traveled to Florida, Rhode Island, Lake Placid. Maeterlinck, who loved seclusion above all else, could not bear the openness, the casual mannerisms, the friendly nature of Americans. At times he even gave vent to his antagonistic feelings; when taken to Harlem to listen to some jazz, he left within five minutes. The discordant sounds were repugnant to him; furthermore, he considered it below his dignity to observe "humanity descending to the levels of monkeys."[151]

Maeterlinck returned to Nice on August 10, 1947. He had grown weaker during the last few years: he had contracted double pneumonia, suffered a broken arm and a fractured knee, and his rheumatism had become increasingly painful. Yet he still walked about his property; still maintained his habits, such as keeping a submachine gun at hand to discourage intruders. He would always shoot into the air first, then, if the prowler was not frightened away, he might discourage his entry in another, more brutal manner.

A year after Maeterlinck's return to France, the French Academy awarded him the "Medal for the French Language." He could never become a member of this august group since he had never become a French citizen. Maeterlinck was prevented from attending the Congress of the P.E.N. Club International in Venice because of a twisted foot.

Life pursued its even course — until May 5, 1949, when Maeterlinck suffered a heart attack. On the following day, at 11 P.M., he entered that atemporal sphere he had described so frequently in his work.

The funeral was held on May 10 in Nice. It was a civil ceremony arranged by the municipality of Nice. There was no priest to perform any religious ritual. To the last, Maeterlinck was true to his word. He did not accept organized religion because it limited the infinite nature of God. He did not fear death since sin and damnation were a figment of man's imagination and never entered into the pleroma of a cosmic divinity.

Maeterlinck's body was cremated in Marseilles.

Words of sympathy were sent from all over the world to his widow.

Maeterlinck does live on in his works — resurrected with every passing generation, each time a new reader or spectator is drawn into his fold!

CHAPTER 6

Conclusion

MAETERLINCK'S plays are unique. The characters are not the flesh-and-blood human beings of conventional theater. They are, rather, presences, essences, will-less fantasy figures who move with an economy of gesture in an atmosphere of strange stillness amid subdued lights. They glide as if moved by some mysterious extraterrestrial force that compels them to fulfill their cosmic destiny. These haunting beings are essentially tragic. As defined by G. K. Chesterton in *Outline of Sanity:* "A tragedy means always a man's struggle with that which is stronger than man."

To the extent that Maeterlinck's early plays are based on symbols, gestures, and the ritual, they may be considered as ancestors of absurdist theater. The conflict in dramas such as *The Intruder, The Blind, Interior, The Death of Tintagiles,* and *Pelléas and Mélisande* is experienced as an inward journey. The exteriorization of the protagonists' moods and feelings is effected by their physical demeanor and by the incantatory quality of their speech. Maeterlinck's language, punctuated with silences, relies heavily on repetition of sounds and phrases that frequently take on the power of a litany, a melopoeia, rediscovering in this form the original function of language, its supernatural and religious characteristics. Gone are the platitudes and banalities. Words no longer used in their habitual sense usher in a world of magic, arousing a multitude of associations and sensations that act and react viscerally upon the onlooker — not by brash or obvious means but rather by imposed restraints, nuances, and subtleties.

Everything within Maeterlinck's plays works toward a cohesive whole. The drama is tightly structured, adhering to the formulas of French classical theater: unity of time, place, and action. Language, decor, lighting, peripeteia, and gesture flow into one central image.

Its impact, accompanied by powerful feeling tones, has a cumulative effect on the audience; nuances flay; feelings pain — until the weight of the experience becomes almost unbearable.

When Maeterlinck succumbed to forces outside of himself, namely to Georgette Leblanc's powerful personality, he wrote for a reason, a goal, for her. His theater became contrived, unauthentic, and, therefore, ephemeral. It was doomed to failure.

Maeterlinck's writings on mysticism and psychometrics are interesting in that they reflect a countercurrent in the twentieth-century world: the overly scientific, mechanized, and industrial society that gave rise to a growing need for the mysterious, unfathomable, and religious domain. What Maeterlinck had sensed in his writings — a similarity in focus between the meditations of the metaphysician and the work undertaken by the empirical physicist — has become a reality today.

Maeterlinck's early plays, like the fairy tale and the myth, are based on primordial experiences. They live on because they capture and materialize in the work of art the eternal part of man.

Ships that pass in the night, and speak each other in passing,
Only a signal shown and a distant voice in the darkness;
So on the ocean of life, we pass and speak one another,
Only a look and a voice, then darkness again and silence.

Longfellow, *Tales of a Wayside Inn.*

Notes and References

Chapter One

1. Maeterlinck was baptized Mauritius Polydorus Maria Bernardus. He signed his first article, "The Massacre of the Innocents," Mooris Maeterlinck. Thereafter, it was Maurice Maeterlinck.
2. *Bulles Bleues* (Monaco: Editions du Rocher, 1948), p. 34.
3. Ibid., p. 27.
4. Ibid.
5. Ibid. p. 25.
6. Ibid.
7. Ibid., p. 49.
8. Ibid., p. 12.
9. Ibid., p. 83.
10. Ibid., p. 84.
11. Ibid., p. 87.
12. *Morceaux Choisis* (Paris: Nelson, 1933). Introduction by Georgette Leblanc, p. vii.
13. Rodenbach's play, *Le Voile*, was performed at the Comédie-Française in 1894.
14. *Bulles Bleues*, p. 196.
15. W. D. Halls, *Maurice Maeterlinck: A Study of His Life and Thought* (Oxford: Clarendon Press, 1960), p. 13.
16. *Bulles Bleues*, p. 195.
17. John Rewald, *The History of Impressionism* (New York: Museum of Modern Art, 1961), p. 508.
18. Ibid., p. 510.
19. *Bulles Bleues*, p. 196.
20. Ibid., p. 197.
21. Ibid.
22. Ibid., p. 198.
23. Ibid., p. 199.

24. Marcel Postic, *Maeterlinck et le Symbolisme* (Paris: Nizet, 1970), p. 16.

25. Gérard Harry, *Maurice Maeterlinck* (Bruxelles: Charles Carrington, 1909), p. 106. Some of the poems included in *Serres Chaudes* had already been published in *La Jeune Belgique* and in the *Parnasse de la Jeune Belgique*.

26. *Bulles Bleues*, p. 204.

27. Ibid., p. 203.

28. Ibid., p. 205.

29. Halls, p.21.

30. Marie Louise von Franz, *Interpretation of Fairy Tales* (New York: Spring Publications, 1970), I, 3.

31. Ibid., p. 1.

32. Ibid.

33. Una Taylor, *Maurice Maeterlinck* (London: Martin Secker, 1914), pp. 22–26.

34. Jakob Boehme, *Confessions* (Paris: Fayard, 1973), p. 9.

35. Edouard Schuré, *The Great Initiates* (New York: St. George Books, 1961), p. 329.

36. *La Princesse Maleine* (Paris: Bibliothèque Charpentier, 1929), p. 5.

37. Ibid., p. 18.

38. Ibid., p. 8.

39. Ibid., p. 74.

40. Ibid., p. 16.

41. Ibid., p. 10.

42. Ibid., p. 21.

43. Guy Doneux, *Maurice Maeterlinck* (Bruxelles: Palais des Académies, 1961), p. 31.

44. *La Princesse Maleine*, p. 88.

45. Ibid., p. 19.

46. Ibid., p. 23.

47. Ibid., p. 56.

48. Ibid., p. 58.

49. Ibid., p. 104.

50. Ibid., p. 158.

51. Ibid., p. 161.

52. Ibid., p. 27.

53. Ibid., p. 34.

54. Ibid., p. 41.

55. Ibid., p. 64.

56. Ibid., p. 64.

57. Ibid., p. 65.

58. Ibid., p. 64.
59. Ibid., p. 66.
60. Ibid., p. 70.
61. Ibid., p. 28.
62. Ibid., p. 32.
63. Ibid., p. 34.
64. Ibid., p. 204.
65. Ibid., p. 222.
66. *Bulles Bleues,* pp. 202—207
67. Ibid., p. 210.

Chapter Two

1. Evelyn Underhill, *John of Ruysbroeck* (London: J. M. Fent, 1916), p. 245.
2. *Théâtre* (Paris: Bibliothèque Charpentier, 1929), I, 226.
3. Ibid., p. 256.
4. Ibid., p. 261
5. Ibid., p. 245.
6. Ibid., p. 233.
7. Ibid., p. 240.
8. Ibid., p. 251.
9. Ibid., p. 259.
10. Ibid., p. 277.
11. Ibid., p. 225.
12. Ibid., p. 242.
13. Ibid., p. 267.
14. Ibid., p. 233.
15. Marcel Postic, *Maeterlinck et le Symbolisme* (Paris: Nizet, 1970), p. 59.
16. W. D. Halls, *Maurice Maeterlinck* (Oxford: Clarendon Press, 1960), p. 32.
17. John Q. Anderson, *The Liberating Gods* (Coral Gables: University of Miami Press, 1972), p. 22.
18. Gérard Harry, *Maurice Maeterlinck* (Bruxelles: Charles Carrington, 1909), p. 18.
19. Eliphas Lévi, *The Key of the Mysteries* (New York: Samuel Weiser, Inc., 1971), p. 45.
20. James Hillman, "On Senex Consciousness," *Spring* (New York: Spring Publications, 1970), p. 147.
21. Edgar Herzog, *Psyche and Death* (New York: G. P. Putnam's Sons, 1967), p. 164.
22. Ibid., pp. 49—52.

23. Emma Jung, *Animus and Anima* (Zurich: Spring, 1972), p. 57.

24. Ibid.

25. René Guénon, *Le Symbolisme de la Croix* (Paris: 10/18), 1957), p. 89.

26. Gershom G. Scholem, *Major Trends in Jewish Mysticism* (New York: Schocken Books, 1965), p. 218.

27. Guénon, p. 293.

28. C. G. Jung, *The Eranos Yearbooks*, (Princeton: Princeton University Press, 1954), I, 375—415.

29. Maurice Raynal, *History of Modern Painting from Baudelaire to Bonnard* (Geneva: Skira, 1949), p. 93.

30. Virginia Crawford, *Studies in Foreign Literature* (Boston: L. C. Page and Co, 1899), p. 10.

31. John Rewald, *Post Impressionism* (New York: Museum of Modern Art, 1956), p. 163.

32. Marie Louise von Franz, *Interpretation of Fairy Tales* (New York: Spring Publications, 1970), I, 1.

33. *Pelléas and Mélisande* (New York: Henry Holt and Co., 1925), p. 5.

34. Ibid., p. 18.

35. Ibid., p. 19.

36. Ibid., p. 23.

37. Ibid., p. 27.

38. Ibid., p. 29.

39. Ibid., p. 30.

40. Ibid., p. 44.

41. Ibid., p. 50.

42. Ibid., p. 74.

43. Ibid., p. 75.

44. Martin Buber, *Good and Evil* (New York: Charles Scribner's Sons, 1952), p. 89.

Chapter Three

1. *Alladine et Palomides* (Paris: Bibliothèque Charpentier, 1918), p. 156.

2. Ibid., p. 155.

3. Ibid., p. 171.

4. Ibid., p. 174.

5. Ibid., p. 160.

6. Ibid., p. 177.

7. Ibid., p. 179.

8. Ibid., p. 200.

9. Ibid., p. 209.

10. Ibid., p. 209.

11. W. D. Halls, *Maurice Maeterlinck: A Study of His Life and Thought* (Oxford: Clarendon Press, 1960), p. 27.

12. *Intérieur* (Paris: Bibliothèque Charpentier, 1918), p. 233.

13. Jethro Bithell, *Life and Writings of Maurice Maeterlinck* (New York: Scribner's Sons, 1913), p. 75.

14. *Intérieur*, p. 241.

15. Ibid., p. 250.

16. Erich Neumann, *The Great Mother* (New York: Pantheon Books, 1955), p. 157.

17. Una Taylor, *Maurice Maeterlinck* (London: Martin Secker, 1914), p. 157.

Chapter Four

1. W. D. Halls, *Maurice Maeterlinck: A Study of his Life and Thought.* (Oxford: Clarendon Press, 1960), p. 46.

2. Ibid., p. 47.

3. M. Esch, *Oeuvres de Maurice Maeterlinck* (Paris: Mercure de France, 1922), p. 38.

4. *Aglavaine et Sélysette* (Bruxelles: P. Lacomblez, 1909), p. 103.

5. Ibid., p. 106.

6. Ibid., p. 109.

7. Ibid., p. 49.

8. Guy Doneux, *Maurice Maeterlinck* (Bruxelles: Palais des Académies, 1961), p. 104.

9. Ibid.

10. Ibid., p. 146.

11. And so it remained until 1918 when their ideal relationship ended.

12. Macdonald Clark, *Maurice Maeterlinck, Poet and Philosopher* (New York: Frederick Stokes, 1916), p. 58.

13. In 1900 these were included in a new edition published under the title *Quinze Chansons* ("Fifteen Songs") appearing at the end of *Serres Chaudes*.

14. *Le Trésor des humbles* (Paris: Mercure de France, 1926), p. 14.

15. Ibid., p. 18.

16. Ibid., p. 85.

17. *Morceaux Choisis* (Paris: Nelson, 1933), p. 26.

18. Virginia Crawford, *Studies in Foreign Literature* (Boston: L. C. Page and Co., 1899), p. 152–156.

19. Ibid., p. 41.

20. Mrs. Patrick Campbell, *My Life and Some Letters* (New York: Benjamin Blom, 1922), p. 169.

21. Ibid., p. 167.

22. *Ariane et Barbe-bleue* (Bruxelles: Lacomblez, 1909), p. 172.

23. The analogy ends, however, in the second part of the ancient myth, when Theseus takes Ariadne to Naxos and abandons her there.

24. *Ariane et Barbe-bleue*, p. 179.

25. Ibid., p. 199.

26. Ibid., p. 227.

27. *Morceaux Choisis*, p. 67.

28. Ibid., p. 70.

29. Paul Flat, "Le Théâtre idéaliste," *La Revue Bleue*, 10 Octobre, 1903.

30. Robert Bossuat, *Le Moyen Age* (Paris: Del Duca, 1962), pp. 128–30.

31. *Soeur Béatrice* (Paris: Bibliothèque Charpentier, 1925), p. 237.

32. Ibid., p. 239.

33. Ibid., p. 240.

34. Ibid.

35. Ibid., p. 247.

36. Ibid., p. 257.

37. Ibid., p. 261.

38. Ibid., p. 273.

39. Ibid., p. 281.

40. Ibid., p. 263.

41. *Monna Vanna* (Paris: Bibliothèque Fasquelle, 1903), p. 36.

42. Ibid., p. 153.

43. Halls, p. 75.

44. Emma Jung and Marie Louise von Franz, *The Grail Legend* (New York: Putnam's Sons, 1970), pp. 247–50.

45. *Joyzelle* (Paris: Bibliothèque Charpentier, 1927), p. 3. *Joyzelle* has been compared to Shakespeare's *The Tempest* because of the enchanted island and the magician-philosopher Prospero and his sprite Ariel.

46. Ibid., p. 99.

47. Ibid., p. 8.

48. Ibid., p. 102.

49. Bronislaw Malinowski, *Magic, Science and Religion* (New York: A Double Anchor Book, 1954), p. 19.

50. *Joyzelle*, p. 175.

51. Esther Harding, *Woman's Mysteries* (New York: Putnam's Sons, 1971), p. 209.

52. Ibid., p. 70.

53. Ibid., p. 140.

54. *Joyzelle*, p. 18.

55. Ibid., p. 16.
56. Ibid., p. 32.
57. Ibid., p. 37.
58. Ibid., p. 41.
59. Ibid., p. 45.
60. Ibid., p. 48.
61. Ibid., p. 55.
62. Ibid., p. 68.
63. Erich Neumann, *The Origins and History of Consciousness* (New York: Pantheon Books, 1954), p. 310.
64. *Morceaux Choisis* (Paris: Nelson, 1933), p. 90.
65. Ibid., p. 91.
66. Ibid., p. 92.
67. Ibid., p. 105, 124. Maeterlinck's chapter on the dog is particularly touching. An animal, he writes, which understands its "supreme obligations" experiences a certain happiness that will remain foreign to man.

Flowers also play a significant role in *The Double Garden.* They correspond to human emotions; they are extensions of man's psyche. What would "humanity be like if he did not know the flower"?

Sincerity is one of the highest virtues, writes Maeterlinck. It is a necessity in a love relationship; it permits one to analyze one's emotions, one's attitude; it leads to "moral perfection."

Chapter Five

1. W. D. Halls, *Maurice Maeterlinck: A Study of His Life and Thought* (Oxford: Clarendon Press, 1960), p. 74.
2. Maeterlinck went to London to attend Herbert Trench's production of *The Blue Bird.*
3. Archibald Henderson, *European Dramatists* (Cincinnati: Stewart and Kidd Co, 1913), p. 244.
4. *The Blue Bird* (New York: Dodd, Mead Co., 1907), p. 26.
5. Ibid., p. 71.
6. Mme Blavatsky asserted that man has several bodies (physical, astral, mental, causal) and each one corresponds to a certain stage in the development of his mind: emotional, mental, thought, and spiritual.
7. *The Blue Bird*, p. 61.
8. Ibid., p. 80.
9. Ibid., p. 81.
10. Ibid., p. 88.
11. George Ferguson, *Signs and Symbols in Christian Art* (New York: Oxford University Press, 1973), p. 13.
12. *The Blue Bird*, p. 79.

13.   Ibid., p. 105.
14.   Ibid., p. 119.
15.   Ibid., p. 189.
16.   Halls, p. 86.
17.   *Morceaux Choisis* (Paris: Nelson, 1933), p. 172.
18.   Ibid., p. 182.
19.   Halls, p. 21.
20.   Ibid., p. 94.
21.   Ibid. pp. 94—95.
22.   Mark: 16: 9.
23.   *Marie-Magdaleine* (Paris: Bibliothèque Charpentier, 1913), p. 28.
24.   Ibid., p. 50.
25.   Ibid., p. 55.
26.   Ibid., p. 63.
27.   Ibid., p. 71.
28.   Ibid., p. 102.
29.   Ibid., p. 123.
30.   Produced at the Neue Stadttheater in Leipzig and at the Chatelet
in Paris.
31.   Halls, p. 99.
32.   Ibid.
33.   Ibid., p. 103.
Despite the honor bestowed on Maeterlinck, he did not go to Sweden to
receive the prize. He used influenza as an excuse. M. Wauters, the Belgian
Minister to Sweden, accepted it for him on December 10, 1911.
34.   In the summer of 1911, Georgette went to Boston to open in
Pelléas and Mélisande.
35.   *La Mort* was not published in French unti 1913.
36.   Halls, p. 111.
37.   J. F. Fabre, *The Life of the Spider* (New York: Dodd, Mead and
Co., 1915), p. 9
38.   Ibid.
39.   *Our Eternity* (New York: Dodd, Mead and Co., 1913), p. 12.
40.   Ibid., p. 39.
41.   Ibid., p. 48.
42.   Ibid., p. 52.
43.   Ibid., p. 65.
44.   Ibid., p. 73.
45.   Ibid., p. 77.
46.   Ibid., p. 95.
47.   Ibid., p. 157.
48.   Ibid., p. 257.
49.   *L'Hôte inconnu* (Paris: Bibliothèque Charpentier, 1917), p. 69.
50.   Ibid., p. 82.
51.   Ibid., p. 152.
52.   Ibid.

53. Ibid., p. 296.

54. Ibid., p. 297.

55. Ibid., p. 298.

56. Ibid., p. 299.

57. Ibid., p. 300.

58. C. G. Jung, *The Structure and Dynamics of the Psyche* (Princeton: Princeton University Press, 1969), p. 449.

59. C. G. Carus, *Psyche* (New York: Spring Publications, 1970), p. 1.

60. Ibid., p. 63.

61. Ibid., p. 14.

62. C. G. Jung, *Memories, Dreams, Recollections* (New York: Pantheon, 1963), p. 304.

63. *Structures*, p. 480.

64. Ibid., p. 434.

65. Ibid., p. 436.

66. *Memories*, p. 390.

67. *Structures*, p. 551.

68. Arthur Koestler, *The Roots of Coincidence* (New York: Random House, 1972), p. 50.

69. Ibid., p. 106.

70. Ibid., p. 107.

71. Ibid., p. 61.

72. Ibid.

73. Ibid., p. 62.

74. Ibid., p. 70.

75. Ibid.

76. Ibid.

77. Ibid., p. 107.

78. Maeterlinck's articles and speeches were later published in volume form in 1916 under the title *Les Débris de la guerre.*

79. "Le Roi Albert," *Journal,* October 13, 1914, p. 13.

80. "L' Héroïsme," *Figaro,* February 11, 1915.

81. *Daily Mail,* September, 1914, p. 5.

82. Ibid.

83. Ibid.

84. *Le Bourgemestre de Stilmonde* was published in 1919.

85. *Le Bourgemestre de Stilmonde* (Paris: Bibliothèque Charpentier, 1919), p. 92.

86. Ibid., p. 9.

87. Ibid., p. 21.

88. Ibid., p. 210.

89. Ibid., p. 16.

90. *Les Fiançailles,* (Paris, Fasquelle, 1922), p. 17.

91. Ibid., p. 20.

92. Ibid., p. 105.

93. Ibid., p. 132.

94. Ibid., p. 134.
95. Ibid., p. 190.
96. Ibid., p. 216.
97. Walter T. Stace, *The Teachings of the Mystics* (New York: A Mentor Book, 1960), p. 16.
98. Ibid., p. 16.
99. The *Upanishads* date from the tenth century B.C. (Ibid., p. 20.)
100. Ibid., p. 22.
101. Ibid., p. 23.
102. *Les Sentiers dans la montagne*, though written during the war was published only in 1919.
103. *Les Sentiers dans la montagne* (Paris: Fasquelle, 1919), p. 9.
104. Ibid., p. 12.
105. Ibid., p. 213.
106. Ibid., p. 178.
107. Stace, p. 75.
108. Ibid., p. 276.
109. Ibid., p. 289.
110. Ibid., p. 69.
111. Ibid., p. 72.
112. *Les Sentiers dans la montagne*, p. 217.
113. Ibid., p. 218.
114. Ibid., p. 230.
115. Ibid., p. 210.
116. Ibid.
117. Georgette's liaison with the actor Roger Karl began, ironically enough, when she performed in *Mary Magdalene* in March, 1913, at the Nice Casino. It is said that he had been in love with her ever since he first saw her in 1907. During World War I Karl was twice wounded. Their liaison at that time was still active. Maeterlinck was indifferent seemingly to Georgette in 1914. Georgette died in February 1941 at Châlet Rose, Le Cannet, in the South of France. Halls, p. 122.
118. Ibid., p. 124.
119. Ibid., p. 131
120. *The Power of the Dead* was written in California in 1919 and rewritten in 1920 for the theater.
121. *The Power of the Dead* (New York: Century Co, 1923), p. 340.
122. Ibid.
123. *Le Grand Secret* (Paris: Fasquelle, 1921), p. 306.
124. *The Life of the White Ant* (New York: Dodd, Mead and Co., 1930), p. 221.
125. *La Vie des termites* (Paris: Charpentier, 1927), p. 52.
126. Ibid., p. 77.
127. Ibid., p. 21.
128. *La Grande Féerie* (Paris: Charpentier, 1929), p. 94.
129. Ibid., p. 141.

130. Ibid., p. 220.
131. Ibid.
132. Ibid., p. 218.
133. *The Supreme Law* (New York: E.P. Dutton, 1935), p. 152.
134. *Avant le Grand Silence* (Paris: Charpentier, 1934), p. 17.
135. Ibid., p. 77.
136. Ibid., p. 35.
137. *The Hour-Glass* (New York: Frederick A. Stokes Co., 1936), p. 9.
138. Ibid., p. 21.
139. Ibid., p. 56.
140. Ibid., p. 55.
141. Ibid.
142. Ibid., p. 77.
143. Ibid.
144. *The Great Beyond* (New York: Philosophical Library, 1947), p. 5.
145. Ibid., p. 81.
146. Ibid., p. 92.
147. Halls, p. 152.
148. Ibid., p. 111.
149. Ibid., p. 155.
150. *The Miracle of the Mothers* is perhaps the only touching drama Maeterlinck wrote during his late years. The play deals with an American soldier killed in action whose mother has not yet been officially notified of his death. He comes to her in a dream. *The Child who does not Want to be Born*, given at Carnegie Hall in New York and featuring Mme Maeterlinck, is a charming sketch in which a mother, at the time her child is to be born, tries to prepare the unborn child for the painful ordeal of his life to be.
151. Halls, p. 154.

Selected Bibliography

PRIMARY SOURCES

PLAYS
La Princesse Maleine. Paris: Bibliothèque Charpentier, 1929.
L'Intruse. Paris: Bibliothèque Charpentier, 1929.
Les Aveugles. Paris: Bibliothèque Charpentier, 1929.
Les Sept Princesses. Bruxelles: Paul Lacomblez, 1891.
Pelléas et Mélisande. New York: Henry Holt and Co, 1925.
Alladine et Palomides. Paris: Bibliothèque Charpentier, 1918.
Intérieur. Paris: Bibliothèque Charpentier, 1918.
La Mort de Tintagiles. Paris: Bibliothèque Charpentier, 1918.
Aglavaine et Sélysette. Bruxelles: Paul Lacomblez, 1909.
Ariane et Barbe-Bleue. Bruxelles: Paul Lacomblez, 1909.
Soeur Béatrice. Paris: Bibliothèque Charpentier, 1925.
Monna Vanna. Paris: Fasquelle, 1903.
Joyzelle. Paris: Bibliothèque Charpentier, 1927.
L'Oiseau Bleu. Paris: Fasquelle, 1909.
Marie-Magdeleine. Paris: Bibliothèque Charpentier, 1913.
Le Miracle de Saint-Antoine. Paris: Bibliothèque Charpentier, 1920.
Le Bourgmestre de Stilmonde. Paris: Bibliothèque Charpentier, 1920.
Les Fiançailles. Paris: Fasquelle, 1922.
Le Malheur passe. Paris: Fayard: 1925.
La Puissance des Morts. Paris: Les Oeuvres libres, 1926.
Berniquel. *Candide*, 22 juillet, 1926.
Marie-Victoire. Paris: Fayard, 1927.
Juda de Kérioth (scène inédite). Paris: Les Oeuvres libres, 1929.
La Princesse Isabelle. Paris: Fasquelle, 1935.
Jeanne d'Arc. Monaco: Editions du Rocher, 1948.
L'Abbé Sétubal. Paris: Del Duca, 1959.
Les Trois Justiciers. Paris: Del Duca, 1959.
Le Jugement dernier. Paris: Del Duca, 1959.
"Les Miracles des mères" (unpublished).

POEMS

Serres chaudes. Chansons complètes. Paris: Librairie Les Lettres, 1955.

SHORT STORIES

"Le Massacre des Innocents." Paris: *La Pléïade, mai 1886.*
"Onirologie." *La Revue générale,* juin 1889.

MEMOIRS

Bulles Bleues. Monaco: Editions du Rocher, 1948.

ESSAYS

Le Trésor des humbles. Paris: Société du Mercure de France, 1915.
La Sagesse et la Destinée. Paris: Charpentier 1902.
La Vie des abeilles. Paris: Charpentier, 1902.
Le Temple enseveli. Paris: Bibliothèque Charpentier, 1912.
Le Double Jardin. New York: Dodd, Mead and Co, 1904.
L'Intelligence des fleurs. Paris: Bibliothèque Charpentier, 1907.
La Mort. Paris: Fasquelle, 1919.
Les Débris de la guerre. Paris: Bibliothèque Charpentier, 1916.
L'Hôte inconnu. New York: Dodd, Mead and Co. 1914.
Les Sentiers dans la montagne. Paris: Fasquelle, 1919.
Le Grand Secret. Paris: Fasquelle, 1921.
La Vie des termites. Paris: Charpentier, 1927.
La Vie de l'espace. Paris: Charpentier, 1928.
La Grande Féerie. Paris: Charpentier, 1929.
Las Vie des fourmis. Paris: Charpentier, 1930.
L'Araignée de verre. Paris: Fasquelle, 1922.
La Grande Loi. Paris: Fasquelle, 1933.
Avant le Grand Silence. Paris: Fasquelle, 1934.
Le Sablier. Paris: Fasquelle, 1936.
L'Ombre des ailes. Paris: Fasquelle, 1936.
Devant Dieu. Paris: Fasquelle, 1937.
La Grande Porte. Paris: Fasquelle, 1939.
L'Autre Monde ou le Cadran stellaire. Paris: Editions Maison Française,
    1942.
Morceaux Choisis. (Paris: Nelson, 1933).

SECONDARY SOURCES

ANDERSON, JOHN Q. *The Liberating Gods.* Coral Gables: University of
    Miami Press, 1971. Interesting volume with regard to Emerson's
    concepts.
BITHELL, JETHROE. *Life and Writings of Maurice Maeterlinck.* New
    York: Charles Scribner's Sons, 1913. Some helpful comments.

BOEHME, JAKOB. *Confessions*. Paris: Fayard, 1973. An aid to an understanding of mysticism.

BUBER, MARTIN. *Good and Evil*. New York: Scribner's Sons, 1952. Imperative for an understanding of the meaning of good and evil.

CAMPBELL, MRS. PATRICK. *My Life and Some Letters*. New York: Benjamin Bloom, 1922.

CARUS, C. G. *Psyche*. New York: Spring Publications, 1970. An early investigation into the psyche; a precursor to Jung.

CLARK, MACDONALD. *Maurice Maeterlinck Poet and Philosopher*. New York: Frederick Stokes, 1916. Fine analysis of philosophical aspects of Maeterlinck's works.

CRAWFORD, VIRGINIA. *Studies in Foreign Literature*. Boston:. L. C. Page and Co., 1899. Informative study on the theater in France.

DONNEUX, GUY. *Maurice Maeterlinck*. Bruxelles: Palais des Académies, 1961. An excellent study on Maeterlinck.

ESCH, M. *Oeuvre de Maurice Maeterlinck*. Paris: Mercure de France, 1922. Interesting because he knew Maeterlinck.

FERGUSON, GEORGE. *Signs and Symbols in Christian Art*. New York: Oxford University Press, 1973. Informative account of the meaning of certain symbols.

FLAT, PAUL. "Le Théâtre idéaliste." *La Revue Bleue*, October 10, 1903.

FRANZ, MARIE LOUISE. *Interpretation of Fairy Tales*. New York: Spring Publications, 1970. Excellent psychological study of fairy tales.

GUÉNON, RENE. *Le Symbolisme de la Croix*. Paris: 10/18, 1957. Comprehensive work.

HALLS, W. D. *Maurice Maeterlinck: A Study of His Life and Thought*. Oxford: Clarendon Press, 1960. Excellent biographical study of Maeterlinck.

HARDING, ESTHER. *Woman's Mysteries*. New York: G. P. Putnam's Sons, 1971. Excellent psychological study of the woman from earliest to modern times.

HARRY, GÉRARD. *Maurice Maeterlinck*. Bruxelles: Charles Carrington, 1909. Valuable insights by a friend of Maeterlinck.

HENDERSON, ARCHIBALD. *European Dramatists*. Cincinnati: Stewart and Kidd Co., 1913. Detailed study of contributions of Lugné-Poë, etc.

HERZOG, EDGAR. *Psyche and Death*. New York: G.P. Putnam's Sons, 1967. Fine study on the psychology of death.

HILLMAN, James. "On Senex Consciousness." *Spring*. New York: Spring Publications, 1970. Excellent study on the psychology of the aging process.

JUNG, C. G. *The Eranos Yearbooks*. I. Princeton: Princeton University Press, 1954.

————. *The Structure and Dynamics of the Psyche*. Princeton: Princeton University Press, 1954.

————. *Memories, Dreams, Reflections*. New York: Pantheon, 1963. Invaluable for psychological understanding of material.

JUNG, EMMA. *Animus and Anima.* Zurich: Spring, 1972. Excellent study on unconscious image of male and female.

JUNG, EMMA and MARIE LOUISE VON FRANZ. *The Grail Legend.* New York: Putnam's Sons, 1970. Study of psychological meaning of Grail Legend.

KNAPP, BETTINA. *Antonin Artaud Man of Vision.* New York: Avon Books, 1971

KOESTLER, ARTHUR. *The Roots of Coincidence.* New York: Random House, 1972. Excellent study of the latest scientific-psychological discoveries.

LÉVI, ELIPHAS. *The Key of the Mysteries.* New York: Samuel Weiser, Inc., 1971. An analysis of numerology.

NEUMANN, ERICH. *The Great Mother* New York: Pantheon Books, 1955.

———. *The Origins and History of Consciousness.* New York: Pantheon Books, 1954. Excellent study of the psyche.

POSTIC, MARCEL. *Maeterlinck et le symbolisme.* Paris: Nizet, 1970. Study in depth of Maeterlinck's symbolist period.

RAYNAL, MAURICE. *History of Modern Painting from Baudelaire to Bonnard.* Geneva: Skira, 1949. Discussion of Nabis movement.

REWALD, JOHN. *The History of Impressionism.* New York: Museum of Modern Art, 1961. Study of entire art movement in France in the 19th century.

SCHOLEM, GERSHOM G. *Major Trends in Jewish Mysticism.* New York: Schocken Books, 1965. Invaluable study on Jewish Mysticism.

SCHURÉ, EDOUARD. *The Great Initiates.* New York: St. George Books, 1961. Inquiry into Pythagorean mysticism.

STACE, WALTER T. *The Teachings of the Mystics.* New York: A Mentor Book, 1960. Selections from mystical writings.

TAYLOR, UNA. *Maurice Maeterlinck.* London: Martin Secker, 1914. A philosophical inquiry into Maeterlinck's works.

UNDERHILL, EVELYN. *John of Ruysbroeck.* London: J. M. Fent, 1916. Important tracts of this Flemish mystic.

Index